INTERNAL CONSULTANCY
IN THE PUBLIC SECTOR

Other titles in the

Systemic Thinking and Practice Series

edited by David Campbell & Ros Draper
published and distributed by Karnac Books

Bentovim, A. *Trauma-Organized Systems. Systemic Understanding of Family Violence: Physical and Sexual Abuse*

Bor, R., & Miller, R. *Internal Consultation in Health Care Settings*

Campbell, D., Draper, R., & Huffington, C. *Second Thoughts on the Theory and Practice of the Milan Approach to Family Therapy*

Campbell, D., Draper, R., & Huffington, C. *Teaching Systemic Thinking*

Cecchin, G., Lane, G., & Ray, W. A. *The Cybernetics of Prejudices in the Practice of Psychotherapy*

Cecchin, G., Lane, G., & Ray, W. A. *Irreverence: A Strategy for Therapists' Survival*

Daniel, G., & Burck, C. *Gender and Family Therapy*

Draper, R., Gower, M., & Huffington, C. *Teaching Family Therapy*

Fruggeri, L., et al. *New Systemic Ideas from the Italian Mental Health Movement*

Hoffman, L. *Exchanging Voices: A Collaborative Approach to Family Therapy*

Inger, I., & Inger, J. *Co-Constructing Therapeutic Conversations: A Consultation of Restraint*

Inger, I., & Inger, J. *Creating an Ethical Position in Family Therapy*

Jones, E. *Working with Adult Survivors of Child Sexual Abuse*

Mason, B. *Handing Over: Developing Consistency across Shifts in Residential and Health Settings*

Ray, W. A., & Keeney, B. P. *Resource-Focused Therapy*

Smith, G. *Systemic Approaches to Training in Child Protection*

Work with Organizations

Campbell, D., Coldicott, T., Draper, R., & Kinsella, K. *The Systemic Approach with Organizations: A Consultant's Handbook*

Campbell, D., Draper, R., & Huffington, C. *A Systemic Approach to Consultation*

McCaughan, N., & Palmer, B. *Systems Thinking for Harassed Managers*

Credit Card orders, Tel: 071-584-3303; Fax: 071-823-7743

INTERNAL CONSULTANCY IN THE PUBLIC SECTOR
Case Studies

edited by
Clare Huffington & Halina Brunning

Foreword by
Charles Hampden-Turner

Systemic Thinking and Practice Series
Work with Organizations

Series Editors
David Campbell & Ros Draper

London
KARNAC BOOKS

This edition first published in 1994 by
H. Karnac (Books) Ltd.
58 Gloucester Road
London SW7 4QY

British Library Cataloguing in Publication Data

A catalogue record for this book is available from the British Library.

ISBN: 1 85575 054 6

Printed in Great Britain by BPC Wheatons Ltd, Exeter

ABOUT THE EDITORS

CLARE HUFFINGTON M.Sc., P.G.C.E.,A.F.B.Ps.S., C.Psychol., Consultant Clinical Psychologist, Child and Family Department, Tavistock Clinic. Her activities include—Organizing Tutor for "Consultation: A Course for Psychologists"; Co-ordinator of Consultation Requests and Convenor of Consultation Workshop, Child and Family Department; joint author, with Ros Draper and David Campbell, of *A Systemic Approach to Consultation*; external and internal consultant to organizations.

HALINA BRUNNING M.A.(Clin. Psych.), A.F.B.Ps.S., C.Psychol., Consulting and Clinical Psychologist, Richmond, Twickenham, and Roehampton Healthcare NHS Trust. Her actitivies include—Organizing Tutor for "New Roles in the Changing NHS" course for clinical psychologists; internal consultant for projects within her own organization; and external consultant for projects within the public sector.

The editors are co-authors, with Carol Cole, of *The Change Directory* and joint authors of a series of articles on consultancy for DCP Forum; together they have run a variety of training initiatives in the field of consultancy.

CONTENTS

EDITORS' FOREWORD

T his is not yet another book about consultancy, but a timely look at some of the tasks facing professionals in welfare, health, and education in the 1990s. Now is a very uncertain time to be working in the public sector; we are reminded of Prigogine saying: "Change is not the exception but the rule."

The editors of this volume, both of whom are psychologists, have been active in the field of consultancy for many years both as trainers and practitioners, and they have long held an interest in disseminating organizational skills to others working for public institutions. They have invited contributors to scrutinize their own work in order to bring to light the important issues underlying internal consultancy. The nine stories presented by the contributors are united by their theoretical framework, but they offer the reader a diversity of ideas which can be applied in different settings. This is not a "cookbook", and some of the examples have proven more effective than others; however, each chapter helps the reader explore an aspect of systemic practice and apply it to their own work. For example, in chapter four, we are presented with ideas for auditing our work while never losing sight of the position within our own system from which we observe our work.

The book is very much "alive", because it is about real practitioners struggling to do a job of work. The contributors have been brave and frank in describing their own learning process, and the idiosyncrasies of each only adds to our ability to relate warmly to the material being presented. As the Series Editors, our own learning was spurred by a particular gem in the Postscript: the authors' edict to themselves and to us that we must create a context in which our clients can feel curious enough to work with us.

David Campbell
Ros Draper
London
March 1994

FOREWORD

I believe it was Dean Swift who said: "Hell hath no fury as when a friend of both parties tactfully intervenes." For the most part, our ultra-individualistic society has followed his advice and hired "helping strangers" and "external consultants" who have put intellectual detachment ahead of emotional involvement.

Hence it is with great pleasure and admiration that I welcome this book on "helping friends" and "internal consultants" by Clare Huffington and Halina Brunning. Their focus is also unusual. They concentrate on the public sector, very much a poor relation to the private sector in the fashion of our times. Although motivated in part by financial stringency — external consultants cost more than internal consultants — Huffington and Brunning have made a genuine virtue of necessity.

For as the authors show, the internal consultant is more knowledgeable about the system, more aware of local particularities. She or he does not have to pretend to be all-seeing and dynamic in order to justify fees of £2,000 a day, nor be preoccupied by seeming to give value for money by offering instant "solutions". Many such persons fear the "passivity" of listening lest they fail to earn their fee.

But the real pleasure of this book is that the mutual involvement of consultant and client, observer and observed in a shared context, allows the authors to display their skills in system dynamics, and these are considerable. Profitability is at best a crude indicator that benefit has been received by customers. Exceptions are, sadly, numerous. But the veritable nest of feedback loops from the recipient of services proposed by authors and contributors allows for far greater fine-tuning between service providers and recipients. This is more than a consultancy paradigm. It is a paradigm for service provision itself. The consultant models what the system should be doing in the relationship formed.

I have always put systems thinkers in two categories. Those who, despite genuflections towards the interdependence of all system elements, do not include themselves in this view. They stand before an imaginary potter's wheel moulding the clay as it revolves; they are not rotating with what they shape. Then there are those who see the wheel as a merry-go-round, or perhaps a misery-go-round, and realize they must jump on board and risk vertigo. These authors are not afraid to jump onto the turning system; indeed, they define themselves as part of it. Their whole paradigm assumes that they are part of the system they observe, which also experiences them.

The external consultant is autonomous by origin. Having many clients is supposed to make she or he independent of any one. The authors show how the internal consultant can negotiate autonomy and neutrality. Nor is the limited power of the internal consultant a serious handicap — indeed, it may be advantageous. Those who truly understand their system dynamics use not their own power but the force-fields in the system itself. The idea is to use minimalist interventions to achieve optimal results. It is this that vindicates the skill of the system dynamicist.

The authors have developed a "life cycle" of consultative stages from Scouting to Withdrawal that allows all concerned to chart the progress of an intervention. I only hope this type of work can be extended to the private sector, where it is badly needed. Economic growth is now inversely proportional to the number of MBAs, external consultants, and economists! Those who are outpacing us see the organization in the image of the family. When things get tough, an "aunt", "uncle", or "cousin" is brought in to mediate. The trouble with pulling external consultants, like rabbits, from a hat is that they know everything *except* the densely involved context of the actual system!

Charles Hampden-Turner
The Judge Institute of Management Studies,
University of Cambridge

INTERNAL CONSULTANCY
IN THE PUBLIC SECTOR

Introduction

Our aim in this book is to offer a timely perspective on the role and application of internal consultancy within the current context of public sector organizations.

At a time of widespread reform in the organization and management of the Social Services, the NHS, and education, many professionals within these systems feel ill-equipped to implement these changes. Consultancy offered to public sector organizations by consultants who work within them offers those involved an opportunity to take stock and reflect on the relentless process of change. It also presents the possibility of seeking local, tailor-made solutions to problems often created in attempting to implement national policy changes. The value of internal consultancy is that these solutions come from the ground floor, whether this is a duty office, hospital ward, or classroom, rather than in the form of recommendations that may be seen as imposed from outside the system, as can sometimes be the case in external consultancy.

Internal consultancy can also become a vehicle for empowerment, as it can offer involvement and a sense of commitment and ownership to all those participating in the process, including

1

management, practitioners, and service users. It is our hope that this book will be an inspiration to others who are called upon to act as internal consultants in their own organizations.

* * *

The background to this book is that each of us has been involved for some years in consultancy projects, both internal and external to our organizations. In the process of engaging in this work, we have come to realize that consultancy is a difficult and challenging process, but one that enables a creative and effective use of limited professional resources, especially in the current climate in the public sector.

In 1990, we wrote a booklet for psychologists on organizational development and the management of change (*The Change Directory*: Brunning, Cole, & Huffington, 1990) in an attempt to present ideas that we hoped would enable others to become involved in consultancy projects. As a result of writing that booklet and further articles (Brunning & Huffington, 1990b, 1991; Ovretveit, Brunning, & Huffington, 1992), we realized that there was an interest in what consultants actually do, as well as in the ideas underpinning their work. People seemed particularly curious about internal consultancy — that is, consultancy requests that arise from within one's own employing organization.

It might be helpful at this point to distinguish between what we mean by consultation and what we mean by consultancy. By *consultation*, we understand a situation where a consultant enters into a relationship with a client about the management of a specific case (an individual, a group of individuals, or a family); or, indeed, the consultant may enter into a relationship with a family within a framework of consultation rather than therapy (Anderson & Goolishian, 1988). By *consultancy*, we wish to indicate a situation where a consultant enters into a relationship with a client — whether an individual, a group, or an organization — about a work-related issue broader than the management of an individual case. The consultancy might be about developing a management role, about teambuilding, or about integrating two units within the organization. This would also include apparently content-led consultancy such as setting up service evaluation procedures or advising on the needs of people with learning disabilities in the community.

We were aware of literature on consultation within a systemic framework (e.g. Andersen, 1984; Anderson & Goolishian, 1986; Fruggeri, Dotti, Ferrari, & Matteinis, 1985; Green & Herget, 1989a, 1989b; Penn & Scheinberg, 1986, Roberts, Caesar, Perryclear, & Phillips, 1989), but we have been able to find very little on consultancy as defined above, still less on internal consultancy. In view of this, we thought it might be useful to gather together examples of how people actually go about internal consultancy within a systems framework.

Nine practitioners—three from each of the Social Services, the NHS, and the education systems—were invited to share both their attempts to consult to their own organizations, and the outcomes and lessons learned from the process. They have worked with individuals, groups, and larger units or the whole organization.

Our intention was to include clear, concise, and practical accounts of actual pieces of work, guided by the authors' thinking at different stages of the consultancy process. We therefore asked each contributor to write his or her own example following the model of stages in the consultancy process outlined in Diagram 1.

We were particularly interested to hear about how the contributors viewed the role of the internal consultant and how issues arising from this were managed. As part of the outcome of the work, we wanted to hear about how the consultants evaluated their effectiveness and understood the client feedback. We thought it was very important to include not only pieces of work perceived as successful, but also those which resulted in uncertain outcomes. These are included as we believe much valuable learning can be derived from other people's struggles and the lessons learned from them. We invited the authors to share, at the ends of their contributions, the specific and general learning that came for them as consultants from the work.

We have concentrated on internal consultancy in the public sector as we are both employed in and familiar with it, and therefore most of our experience is derived from this field. We also note that public sector organizations are currently undergoing profound changes. These affect customary methods of service delivery, question traditional assumptions, and challenge existing power relation-

1. Scouting :

Change Agent decides whether or not to 'enter' the system.

6. Planning :

Identifying specific interventions, including who will do what, and how it might be evaluated.

2. Entry :

Establishing a relationship with the client as a basis for further involvement.

7. Intervention :

Carrying out the planned implementations.

3. Contracting :

Developing a mutual contract, clarifying expectations and *modus operandi*.

8. Evaluation :

Assessing the success of the interventions and the need for further action or withdrawal.

4. Data Gathering:

Measuring organisational indices and variables.

9. Withdrawal :

If no further action by the change agent is required, managing the termination of the OD work, while at the same time leaving the system with an enhanced capacity to manage such change by itself, in the future.

5. Diagnosis :

Interpreting the data, feeding it back to the client and developing a joint understanding.

Change Agent = Consultant; OD = Organizational Development

Source: Brunning et al. (1990), *The Change Directory*. Diagram reprinted with the kind permission of Kristof Bien.

DIAGRAM 1: *Key stages in the consultancy process*

ships to the point that a rich internal market for consultancy projects is created (see chapter one).

Parts two, three, and four contain the contributions from the nine practitioners and deal with internal consultancy within, respectively, the Social Services, the NHS, and education, with a brief introduction at the beginning of each part on organizational issues facing each of these systems. It is important to note that all contributors have addressed the issue of confidentiality, and details that might identify people or places have been changed.

In the Postscript, we have drawn together themes emerging from the case studies, together with lessons we have learned in the process of consultancy projects and from reading about other people's endeavours.

We begin in part one with some theoretical issues about internal consultancy within a systemic framework, starting by setting the scene in the public sector of the 1990s.

INTERNAL CONSULTANCY IN CONTEXT

CHAPTER ONE

The current context in the public sector

L et us begin by defining what we mean by the public sector. It is used to be simple to define it as welfare and other public services owned by the state and financed by taxation, such as roads, railways, health, education, and Social Services; or where public purchasing determined the nature and infrastructure of an organization—for example, special boarding schools or homes for the elderly. Another way to define the public sector would be by describing facilities in public ownership—buildings, equipment, etc. However, over the past 10 years, the public sector has changed so much that these definitions no longer fully apply. For example, NHS Trusts are quasi-independent but still in public ownership. Even the concept of profit no longer distinguishes the public and private sectors; NHS Trusts have to make at least 6% return on their capital. As the "mixed economy" of public and private financing evolves, the concept of the public sector is thus losing its previous definition. Perhaps the safest and simplest way to define it at present is in terms of the proportion of public income used: those services that depend for their existence largely on public contracts and financing and where the buildings and equipment are also within public ownership.

Over the past decade, the public sector has been undergoing unprecedented changes, such that the current culture is one of discontinuous but constant change. This has led to stress and problems in various parts of the system, leading to requests for help—for example, Social Services departments having to decide how to manage drastically reduced budgets and contract with private and voluntary providers, NHS managers faced with hospital closures, schools with not enough staff to teach children with special needs. All these may lead to requests for help from consultants.

Public sector organizations are now more tightly managed on a local basis, and the purchaser/provider model is being adopted across the board. This brings with it notions of increased responsiveness to the consumers' needs and service quality (see Ovretveit, 1992). Both concepts concern the creation of feedback loops between consumers and providers of services so as to create the most effective services to meet the needs. Local knowledge is highly valued in this culture.

At the moment, however, it seems that, whereas some professionals are being pushed towards the direct client contact or "provider" parts of their roles (e.g. psychologists), others are being pushed away from it into "purchaser" roles (e.g. social worker to care manager). Teamwork and inter-agency cooperation are, however, being stressed, to ensure that the services are bought and cost-effectiveness is maximized. It may appear that holding on to or developing work at a meta level such as consultancy will be very difficult. Despite the similarity to the private sector, we think consultancy in this newly defined public sector will differ in several important ways from private sector consultancy, and the consultant will need to consider carefully the following:

- issues of costing, if not profit—what fees are "reasonable" and necessary to survive in the "contract culture";
- development and marketing of new services, giving consumers information on which to make choices, rather than selling an

image or dream—how to manage expectations and where to draw the line in a competitive climate;

- how to manage staff through change processes without using the whole-scale redundancies of private sector organizations under pressure;
- advising purchasers on keeping services at the cutting edge in the internally controlled market mainly by cooperation, not by cut-throat competition with other services.

Whereas public sector organizations used to turn to external consultants for help with managing change, they appear to be becoming sceptical about the value of commercial consultancies, many of whom do not understand the public sector and offer expensive, packaged solutions with which the organization cannot engage. They seem to be turning to consultants from within the organization to provide ongoing help in the management of change.

There are many tasks arising from the cultural and structural changes in the public sector with which the internal consultant could help: for example, with the creation of user groups, quality circles, models for inter-agency working, and new multi-disciplinary teams; helping to shape policy and decision-making processes for purchasers: helping with the creation of preventative services; and many other examples of indirect facilitative work via teachers, nurses, social workers, and others. Hence there is a great need for professionals within public sector organizations to consolidate and develop consultancy skills, as well as to market these effectively within the new organizational culture.

As we have commented in an earlier article (Ovretveit et al., 1992), the problem in putting oneself forward as a resource within the organization may come as much from ambivalence in the potential consultant as from the kind of organizational constraints described above. This ambivalence may arise from a personal and professional belief system at odds with the market economy culture in the changing public sector. The issue is therefore one of legitimacy: whether engaging in consultancy can be seen as part of a set of beliefs about one's professional role in this new organizational culture. This is a dilemma for the potential consultant, for the consultant's manager, and for other members of the consultant's professional group to address and resolve. Some of the case studies presented here deal explicitly with this process of negotiating legitimacy for internal consultancy as an essential prerequisite of being able to take on the work.

CHAPTER TWO

Internal consultancy: theoretical issues

A DEFINITION OF CONSULTANCY

Let us start with another definition: consultancy is a process involving a consultant who is invited to help a client with a work-related issue. The client can be an individual, a group, or an organization. The essential issue is one of responsibility for the process, and this may help to clarify the difference between consultancy and other activities, such as supervision, therapy, teaching, and management. The responsibility for *fulfilling the task* of the organization in the consultancy process lies with the client, whereas the responsibility for the consultancy *process* lies with the consultant. The consultant uses his or her skills and knowledge about the process of change to enter into a mutual exploration towards an understanding of the meaning of the problem for the organization as a whole. The consultant's position within the system offers a different perspective from that of the client. From this perspective, the consultant can offer new ideas that may create a new set of meanings in the organization and allow the problem to be seen in a different way, leading to new behaviours and new relationships. These may allow the organization to move forward in its development.

The consultant may work with many different kinds of problem, from working with nurses on how to manage bereavement to helping a community care team to develop an operational policy. The consultant may act in different roles at various stages of the process—for example, as teacher, advisor, facilitator, researcher, troubleshooter, salesperson—without letting go of the locus of responsibility. As well as being able to take on a variety of roles to suit the overall task, the consultant needs to be able to move quickly between them, whilst maintaining a bird's eye view of both the primary task to be accomplished and the whole system involved in the project.

The consultant working within a systemic framework will use specific techniques such as hypothesizing, circular questioning, and the use of feedback and reflective discussion. The aim is to create a context in which new ideas can be owned—in the sense of feeling a commitment towards—by the client, whose responsibility it is to implement any resulting actions. The practice of consultancy within a systemic framework is described in detail in an earlier book in this series (Campbell, Draper, & Huffington, 1991b), to which the reader should refer if unfamiliar with this approach. Bor and Miller (1991) in another book in this series provide an excellent theoretical and practical account of internal consultancy in health care settings using a systemic framework.

EXTERNAL AND INTERNAL CONSULTANCY

External consultancy involves consultancy to individuals, groups, or organizations outside the organization of which the consultant is a member. Internal consultancy, on the other hand, involves consultancy to individuals, groups, or the whole organization of which the consultant is also a member. As we have suggested (in chapter one), requests for consultancy from one's own organization are likely to become increasingly common in the public sector of the 1990s. For some professionals in the public sector, this kind of work is already an integral part of the job.

What the internal consultant can offer is local knowledge and "coming in at the ground floor". This means the possibility of spotting the need for consultancy early on. This can allow the consultant to facilitate the growth of a broad base of support for change, which in turn can help the organization own the consequences of a change effort. Many attempts at external consultancy fail at this implementation stage, when the organization needs to own an intervention sufficiently to be able to put it into daily practice. Could it be that the act of hiring an external consultant is a way for the organization to distance itself from the need to change? Certainly, it seems that the fact that public sector organizations now allow and encourage staff to offer internal consultancy services suggests an ownership of the need for the organization to change itself rather than a reliance on others to do it from outside. This is said to be one of the characteristics of the "healthy organization" (Harrison & Robertson, 1985). In any case, where the consultancy is conducted from within, the implementation of any changes has a better chance of succeeding as the need for change has been owned by the organization from the start by employing an internal consultant and requesting help from that person.

Another advantage for the internal consultant is that the work costs less, and this is very important in today's cost-conscious environment. There are many recent examples of expensive mistakes made with external consultants. Therefore, public sector organizations are now looking within for help with organizational problems.

Internal consultancy, however, presents specific dilemmas which need careful consideration before accepting requests for help. Bianco (1985) says of internal and external consultants: "The internal wishes for the freedom of the external and the external wishes for the continuity of the internal." She also points out that the internal consultant may have far more knowledge and access to internal resources, power figures, history, and so on. These apparent benefits may, however, work to the internal consultant's disadvantage in that the consultant may not find it so easy to develop new ideas to deal with stuck situations. It is clear that the internal consultant faces both opportunities and challenges and these are discussed in the remainder of this chapter.

THE OBSERVER POSITION

In requesting the help of a consultant about an organizational problem, the client is simultaneously creating a new context (or set of
expectations) of an observed system (Von Foerster, 1979): that the
problem will be observed by a person "outside" the immediate
system (see Diagram 2). This is, on the face of it, the position of the
internal consultant.

This context, however, consists of expectations in the observed
or client system about being observed as having a problem. In
addition, behaviour that results from being observed as having a
problem may have developed. For example, the manager and
deputy of a children's home, who have asserted that they do not get
on, have asked their line manager for a consultant to help them with
their relationship. Having done this, they may spend a lot of time
avoiding each other in the belief that they will make the problem
worse if they talk together.

The observer, or consultant, has his or her own sets of expectations about problems in organizations in general, about the specific
referred problem, and about behaviour that is related to solving
problems. Together, the observer and observed are part of a "problem-determined system" (Anderson & Goolishian, 1986). This

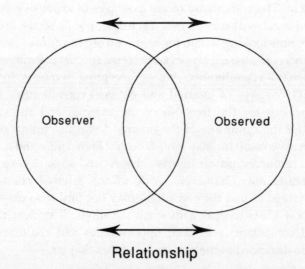

DIAGRAM 2: *The observed system*

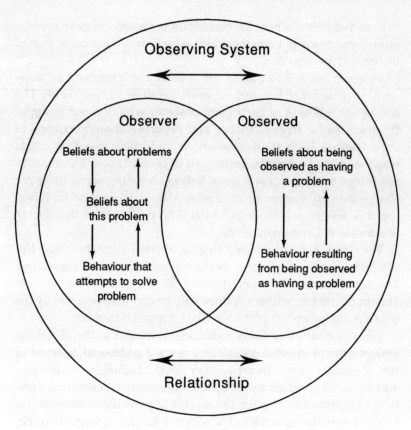

DIAGRAM 3: *The observing system*

second-order cybernetics position (Von Foerster, 1979; Hoffman, 1985) is represented in Diagram 3.

The shift from the model of an observed to an observing system means recognizing that the consultant is part of the system being observed, and that the consultant's objectivity is then limited by this context (Mendez, Caddou, & Maturana, 1988). This is the case whether the consultant is "external" or "internal" to the organization requesting help.

Problems can, however, occur if there is a belief that the consultant *can* be outside the system, whether or not the consultant is employed inside or outside the organization. If this belief persists, then what follows can be a hierarchical relationship between consultant and client, where the consultant is thought to have *superior* knowledge or insight into the problem by virtue of not being part of the immediate situation.

In seeing oneself as part of the system, the consultant is, however, in a *different* but not superior position to the client. The consultant is a kind of participant observer who does not bring as the main tool a map of theory and expertise about problems in organizations; rather, the consultant and client together create maps as part of a creative endeavour of co-evolution. The consultant brings to the process a set of beliefs about the possibilities for change in every system, stuck or otherwise, and a method for bringing this about via a dialogue with different parts of the system (Anderson & Goolishian, 1988).

The observing system involving an internal consultant may imply different meanings from that involving an external consultant. The exploration of the expectations of the consultancy as a whole is very important as, without it, there may be confusion created by the overlapping meanings of the internal/external dimension.

What is even more likely to become confused in the observing system around internal consultancy are the additional contexts or sets of expectations of therapy, supervision, teaching, management, and so on, all of which may be part of the internal consultant's role in the organization at other times. This is particularly relevant for internal consultants in the public sector, who almost without exception have generic roles related to the fulfilment of basic professional roles, such as teaching, therapy, or management. The internal consultancy role is an additional, usually time-limited, negotiated role in relation to specific tasks or projects.

The specific discipline or professional background of the consultant may add to the multiplicity of contexts involved in the consultancy. For example, a psychiatrist acting as a staff group consultant may find the staff group worried about whether the consultant will be diagnosing the pathology of the staff group members. Also, the hierarchical relationship between the consultant and client may or may not facilitate collaborative work. All these issues would lead to different kinds of observing systems. If, however, the internal consultant is able to manage moving between different roles in an organization, this may model for its members the process of being able to take on different roles for different tasks which are sometimes quite independent from one another. This can be useful for staff teams stuck around the issue of difference. Another advantage is that acting as an internal consultant may act to facilitate rather than hinder the performance of other aspects of a consultant's role in an organization.

Since problems could be seen to result from conflicts between contexts or an experience of "bad fit" between beliefs or constructs about experience and experience itself (Campbell et al., 1991a), then the first stage of the consultancy process may be to clarify expectations about the multiple contexts in relation to the consultancy. As Nufrio (1983) points out, lack of clarity can lead to a feeling of "madness" (or totally confused contexts!) in the internal consultant unless the various roles and activities being undertaken at each stage are clarified. The roles and activities need to be explained and understood by participants in the process. For example, one might ask in a piece of consultancy around teambuilding in a Social Services department area team, "What does it mean to be teamleader that the consultant is observing the work of the family aides at this stage of the process?" "How do they think this activity is connected to the task of the consultancy?" As Pace and Argona (1989) say, the internal consultant needs a high tolerance of ambiguity as well as a sense of humour and an appetite for a challenge!

NEUTRALITY

In an organization negotiating change, individuals and the organization as a whole will be dealing with challenges to accepted beliefs, associated behaviours, and relationships. In the public sector, the new organizational culture may lead people to feel themselves under threat of losing their jobs. At times such as these, a consultant may be brought in with the aim of binding the consultant to the view of the problem held by the client, perhaps to prevent loss of influence, keeping the system in standstill (Selvini-Palazzoli, 1980; Anderson & Goolishian, 1988; Williams, 1989). The client may, however, believe that, in consulting someone outside the situation (even if not completely external), this person can be impartial or more objective than those immediately involved. This may, in the NHS setting, fit with beliefs about impartiality being a necessary component of good clinical practice (Bor & Miller, 1991).

The internal consultant's view of the problem will, however, inevitably be affected by the conflicts about change being shared at that time by everyone in the organization; whether, for example, the changes in question are a "good" or "bad" thing. This will include the beliefs in the organization about the process of change which legitimized the consultant undertaking pieces of consultancy work. For example, there may be a belief that parts of the organization need not be responsible for sorting out their own organizational problems but should seek the help of the consultant to the organization; or that the consultant needs to be given work to make sure the "real" work of management is not impeded; or that the organization gets on best if it is in a state of internal competition, and help from a consultant is needed only if the competition spills over into serious conflict. There are many other possible hypotheses that need to be developed at the stage of receiving a request for consultancy to try to understand the meaning of the problem for the organization.

It may be relevant to consider whether the person making the request (the client or referrer) had a choice of approaching an external or internal consultant, and how the decision was made to approach an internal consultant (see Diagram 4). It may be important to think about the relationship in the organizational structure between the referrer and the consultant. In Diagram 4, the Manager of Team 3 in Organization 1 is approaching a consultant who is also a member of Team 2. It may be that the referrer expected to be more able to bind the consultant to his or her point of view because of their shared membership of the same organization and hierarchy; both are also accountable to the same Unit Manager. The referrer in the diagram, who is also a manager, may assume, because this position is superior in the hierarchy to the consultant, that the consultant is more likely to agree with the referrer's point of view.

Other people in the organization—for example, members of Teams 1, 2, and 3 and depending on whether or not they are the subjects of the consultancy—will interpret the actions of the consultant in a similar way; that is, they may assume that the internal consultant has been brought in to support the positions and policies of those who created the post of internal consultant (e.g. the Unit Manager), or those who referred the problem (Manager of Team 3). Anyone involved with the internal consultant will wonder: "Whose

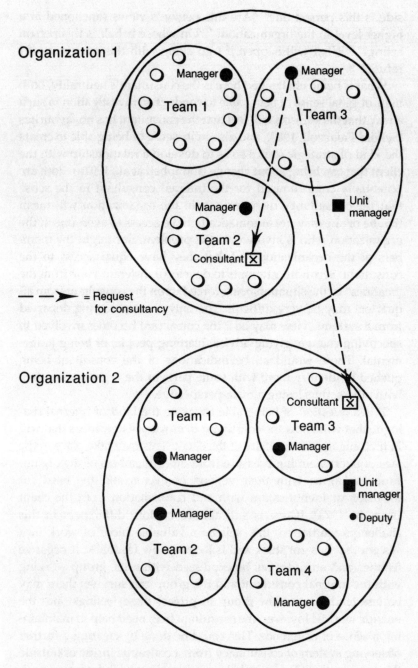

DIAGRAM 4: *External and internal consultancy.*

side is this person on?" "Are this person's views sanctioned at a higher level in the organization?" "On whose behalf is this person acting?" "What will happen if I go along with this person, or if I refuse?"

What is being challenged here is the consultant's neutrality, both in its original sense of being able to conduct an investigation in such a way that the subjects will feel that the consultant has no favourites (Selvini-Palazzoli, 1980); and also in its sense of being able to create the kind of strategic stance so as to develop a relationship with the client that can bring about change (Campbell et al., 1991a). Both are potentially compromised for the internal consultant in the sense that the consultant's own position in the organization will mean that he or she may not automatically have access to everyone in the organization who is involved in the problem, nor might the members of the organization feel that they have equal access to the consultant. Secondly, attempts to develop a different view from the "realities" of the situation being forced upon the consultant from all quarters may be very difficult. The only clues of having departed from a systemic view may be if the consultant becomes involved in specifying change, giving advice, blaming people, or being judgemental. These would all be indications of the consultant being pushed to identify more with some parts of the organization than with others, thus losing a meta-perspective.

It is a question of being able to create the kind of internal dialogue that will allow the consultant to introduce new ideas that will in turn engage the curiosity of the client. This may take place in the face of overwhelming pressure from other members of the organization to agree with their version of events and the need for inclusion or identification with and confirmation from the client (Argyris, 1973). If one is still able to explore differences in this challenging situation, this will be a valuable piece of work in a system that has got stuck and is lacking new feedback. If negative feelings and attitudes *can* be expressed within the group working with the internal consultant and the group can survive, there may be less tendency for the group to project these feelings onto the outside world. However, the consultant may need help in maintaining a sense of difference. This could be done by creating a further observing system of consultancy from a colleague inside or outside the organization. This may help to maintain the kind of meta-position needed to develop new ideas and also give another perspective on which levels of identification with the client will help and which will hinder the achievement of the consultancy task.

The struggle to remain meta may be most difficult in consulting to the members of one's own team. In Diagram 4, this would mean a situation in which members of Team 2 approached the consultant, also based in Team 2, for help with a problem within the same team. One is then dealing with the conflicting contexts of belonging to a team, which means sharing a common view of the "realities", and having different views which might perturb the system into change. This could lead to potential conflicts of loyalty, which might threaten the legitimacy of the role of consultant, of team member, and of the task of consultancy itself. It may be that the feedback loop is too small to allow differences to be explored. Perhaps the best clue to whether it is possible is how curious one feels as a consultant. Looking at Diagram 4, the consultant could consult to Team 1 or 3, but it is not clear whether it would be possible to do so for Team 2. The curiosity factor may or may not be present. If it is not and it is not possible to negotiate to a different consultancy task that will engage the consultant and the client, a consultant more external to the team may be needed.

CONSTRAINT AND AUTONOMY

Members of an organization have areas where they can perform autonomously and areas of constraint—for example, lines of accountability and responsibility. This situation is usually enshrined in a job description. We think that people in an organization tend to perform most effectively where there is a fit between the autonomy and the constraints they will accept in order to be part of that organization. If people feel too autonomous, they may not have enough of a sense of belonging to the organization; if, on the other hand, they feel too controlled, it may be impossible to make an individual creative contribution (see Diagram 5).

The consultant also has areas where he or she expects autonomy: for example, in the management of the consultancy process, including the methods to use, access to people in the significant system around the problem, pacing, etc. In order to function effectively, the consultant also needs the framework of an agreed contract sum-

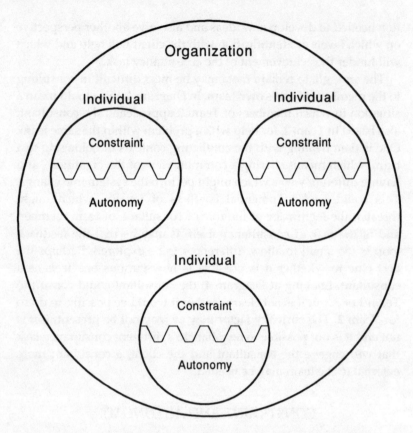

DIAGRAM 5: *Constraint and autonomy in the organization*

marizing aims, objectives, time scale, feedback, and the evaluation mechanisms, etc.

It is clear that the client may often request the help of the internal consultant in order to defend against loss or to maintain the drift of behaviour in a desired direction. For example, a headteacher may request consultancy for a staff group in the belief that this may stem rebellion and challenges to his or her authority. The request may be made in a way that places constraints on the behaviour of the consultant and makes it an impossible task to perform.

For example, a consultant was invited to assist a personnel section in a Social Services department in a project aimed at "selection or de-selection" of staff for a particular project. This request seemed to imply the use of a consultant's expertise to facilitate others to exert control within the organization. It might have been possible to enter into an exploration of the reasons for this particular request and the confused contexts implied by it. A new understanding of the organizational conflicts represented by the request might have emerged and, from this, an alternative strategy for solving the problem. For example, the consultant might have been able to reframe the task as facilitating managers with staff development—and out of this might have come the beginnings of an appraisal scheme from which it would be possible to see which staff needed and wanted opportunities to work in new projects. However, this proved impossible; the consultant was constrained about which people could be interviewed and in which combinations, the questions that could be asked, and the kinds of recommendations that would be acceptable at the end of the process. The constraints placed upon the autonomy of the internal consultant in this situation meant that the consultant stood little chance of making a difference, and the request was therefore turned down. In fact, most internal consultants find themselves refusing some requests, for this or similar reasons. However, the internal consultant may find that, when it is not possible to be involved as a consultant, the context that emerges may be a different one in which it *is* possible to function effectively, for example in one's own discipline role or as a manager. With the above reframe, a consultant in role as a manager could start discussion of an appraisal scheme with members of his or her staff group. This might have a ripple effect on other groups, which could eventually lead to change in the organization as a whole.

The beginning stages of the consultancy process are thus vital to being able to negotiate a position from which one can bring about change. As in the example above, a request can be presented in a form that feels too constraining to allow the exploration of differences: one may feel that one is being forced to accept a role that fits with the view that the person making the request has about the organization, but which may not allow change to occur. One needs to be highly attentive to the way an initial request is framed, in that it indicates how the person making the request wants to organize the consultant so as to fit his or her "story". It is our experience also that the consultant can often feel rushed into a commitment to act before having time to think. We think that time taken at this stage to hypothesize around the meaning of the request is time well spent. The nature and wording of the request itself can give valuable information about conflicting beliefs in the organization.

For example, a request for teambuilding from the manager of a children's home and his line manager was coupled with complaints that one of the staff was very difficult to manage and quite unruly in the staff group. In an initial meeting with these two managers, it became apparent that both of them lacked clarity about their management tasks and that they were being expected to care for children without any clear expectations or structure about the task. So the request about teambuilding, or care for the staff, and the need to control an unruly member of staff reflected the actual conflict between care and control which was at the root of the managers' difficulties with the client group in the organization as a whole. In fact the group of teenagers in the home presented a challenge that mirrored this dilemma — the need to care for and to control them. Looked at in this way, it seemed helpful to spend a number of sessions working with the managers on the kind of expectations they might have of more senior managers for policy and guidelines and how these might be discussed with the staff. Teambuilding work seemed quite a long way down the road, but still possible later on, given this initial reframing of the task.

POWER ISSUES

This leads us into considering the significance of power issues. Winn (1973) points out that internal consultants are invariably placed in low-status staff positions with no legitimate influence. The internal consultant is therefore often faced with the need to create credibility through the success of work undertaken. As Bianco (1985) comments, however, the internal consultant is trapped in a Catch-22 situation. If actions are perceived as too cautious, the internal consultant can be treated as "an extra pair of hands". If actions are perceived as challenging the status quo, the internal consultant can be seen as disloyal or insensitive to the organization and risks being scapegoated.

If, however, the consultant can think carefully about the reason for the request of consultancy, taking into account power relationships, then it may be possible to arrive at a strategy that will engage participants in a co-evolving process. At the end of it, people may be able to say, "We did it ourselves!" Alternatively, the consultant may feel that the performance of the task of consultancy will be so constrained, as described in the previous section, that the request is best refused.

Let us now turn to informal power, specifically inequalities of gender, culture, class, and disability in public sector organizations and their relevance to internal consultancy.

All these variables can be argued to be "irreducible categories" of human life, rather than secondary or mediating variables (see Goldner, 1988, on gender) or the product of "linguistic error" (Bateson, 1973). Organizations are typically described in structural and hierarchical terms (e.g. Handy, 1981), and usually these descriptions are reconstituted within dominant white, male, and middle-class cultural terms. This also includes the role of internal consultant. It tends to lead to a context in which inequalities of power in the form of gender, class, culture, and disability are considered to be personal, non–work-related contexts, too sensitive for examination, and "forbidden territory". This might lead the internal consultant into consulting only with those with the most powerful voices in the organization — probably the white, male, middle-class ones. It is as if developing a dialogue about inequalities might lead to a redistribution of feelings of powerlessness even more uncomfortable than those feelings of powerlessness around the original consultancy problem referred. This difficulty is also likely to be connected to the nature of the public sector client group, including some of the least powerful and most deprived members of society. In this sense, issues of inequality have a highly significant relationship to the primary task of the organization and hence to the consultancy, the purpose of which, in the end, is to facilitate this task.

In order to engage in systemic consultancy, the consultant will need to involve all participants in the problem-determined system in a co-evolving process in which the consultant with "respectful curiosity" can ask people about their view of the problem (Cecchin, 1987). This must involve developing the kind of dialogue that includes perspectives from the least to the most powerful in the system, regardless of position in the hierarchy. This will include women, members of different cultures, classes, ages, and disabilities. The consultant may need to adopt a strategic stance that will positively encourage these voices, whilst restraining those voices which are otherwise heard most often (Fisher, personal communication 1992). This will mean the consultant shedding power so as to empower others to speak and allow new ideas to develop (Hoffman, 1988). This will be particularly difficult for the internal consultant whose role has been constituted within the conservative organizational culture, which may not give its members this autonomy.

However, the culture in the public sector is changing from a relatively poor relationship with the outside world to one in which it is essential to be able to react to consumer need and choice in order to survive: the consumer, rather than the manager, rules! Employee participation, together with management commitment and support, has been shown to be associated with successful large-scale organizational change undertaken by internal consultants (Pace & Argona 1989; Covin & Kilmann, 1990a, 1990b). Many public sector organizations will be wanting to discover how to respond effectively to consumers, many of whom will be the most disadvantaged in society. If there is to be a successful process of setting up a reflexive loop between consumer and service provider, some fundamental changes in management and structures within the organization will be required. An example is the implementation of equal opportunities policies, which have profound implications at all levels of organizational functioning, from first contact with a client to the running of the boardroom. The nature of the Patients' Charter in the NHS, for example, has this as its primary intent.

First steps towards meeting the needs of this outward-facing organizational culture will entail the improvement of responsiveness within the organization to feedback from consumers which reaches the lowest levels of the organization first, through those in direct contact with consumers. Organizations will need to learn to listen to their front-line workers, who are the people in the organization most likely to be women, from ethnic minorities, the working class, the disabled, and so on. The formal hierarchy is thus being reversed in the search for a market lead, but organizations may turn to internal consultants for help with how to achieve it. Clearly, there are many dilemmas that may follow in this tension between management and consumer power.

OUTCOME MEASUREMENT

There are relatively few studies that look at the effectiveness of systemic interventions. Those studies we know of relate to family therapy interventions (e.g. Bennun, 1986; Mashal, Feldman, & Sigal, 1989; Carr, 1991) or consultation (e.g. Green & Herget, 1989a, 1989b), but not consultancy, still less internal consultancy. What is desperately needed as a start is an attempt to audit consultancy work in simple terms, including outcome measures of some kind. The issue of outcome measurement, reframed as the formal use of feedback, should not be too problematic for consultants working in a systemic framework. The use of feedback is essential at all stages of consultancy to give meaning to the process as it evolves. The task of evolving outcome measure would therefore seem to involve creating some formal mechanisms for measuring change within the feedback process. The essence of this approach would be that what is seen as "good practice" would be generated by the participants in the process.

The definition of these outcome measures could be part of the initial context-marking dialogue around consultancy. This might involve asking certain questions of the client and of oneself as consultant. For example:

- What changes do you expect to see if the consultancy is effective?
    (a) at individual level—staff and users;
    (b) at group level—staff and users;
    (c) at system or service level — e.g. user numbers seen, speed of administration, money saving, pupil achievements.
- How can these changes be operationally defined?
- How will you measure these changes and when?
    (a) informal discussion;
    (b) interview or questionnaire;
    (c) formal tests — e.g. patient depression level.
- What will you do if the consultancy does not bring about these changes?
- Which aspects of the consultancy process were most helpful and unhelpful; challenging; etc.?

- What did you learn from the experience?
- What would constitute bad practice in this case?

Lippitt and Lippitt (1978) suggest some useful ideas on evaluating consultancy. Also, Ovretveit offers guidelines on developing quality services in the public sector in general in his 1992 book, *Health Service Quality*.

CHAPTER THREE

Internal consultancy: practical considerations

So what do all these dilemmas mean for the practice of internal consultancy? It seems to us that they go some way to creating the kind of internal dialogue that the consultant needs to have in order to facilitate the dialogue that will take place with members of the organization. We have therefore listed questions that might spark off this dialogue under each of the areas discussed in chapter two.

1. *The observer position*
   - What are the expectations of the consultant?
   - If these expectations are confused with those more appropriate to other activities — for example, therapy, teaching, or other discipline roles — then how will you explore this?
   - How might expectations be different if the consultant was external to the system?
   - What do you need to do to set up a collaborative relationship with the client?

- How will you ensure the maintenance of an internal dialogue so as to keep a meta-perspective throughout the process?

2. *Neutrality*
   - What is under threat from change in the organization?
   - How is the referring person under threat; what might he or she be losing?
   - What are the expectations of the consultant in relation to this threat?
   - What are the beliefs about the process of change in the organization, including beliefs about the creation of the consultant's role?
   - What is the relationship between the consultant and the client in the organizational structure? What is the relationship with other parts of the organization?
   - How will you know you have departed from a systemic view?

3. *Constraint and autonomy*
   - Where are the areas of constraint and autonomy in the organization for the individuals in it, particularly the referrer?
   - Where are the areas of autonomy of the consultant?
   - Will the consultant have sufficient autonomy to be able to achieve the task within the context of consultancy?
   - In what circumstances would you refuse this request for consultancy?

4. *Power issues*
   - How does the organization speak and act about issues of gender, culture, class, disability?
   - How might these issues be connected to the referred problem?
   - What kind of strategic stance will you need to take to create a dialogue with all participants in the consultancy process about these issues?

5. *Outcome measurement*
- How could you audit the process of the consultancy?
- What kinds of questions would you need to ask to be able to get feedback about the effectiveness of the consultancy?
- What will count as success and what as failure in the consultancy task?
- What will happen if you succeed with the task, or if you fail?

With these questions in mind, we would now like to present our selection of case studies.

PART TWO

INTERNAL CONSULTANCY
IN THE SOCIAL SERVICES

Introduction

Thurstine Basset
Independent Training Consultant

Social Services departments are relatively young, having been set up in 1971 as an amalgamation of three existing departments: Children, Welfare, and Mental Health.

Now, just over 20 years on from their birth, the main question is whether they will survive the 1990s at all.

Throughout their existence, Social Services departments have struggled with various questions that directly determine how services are delivered. One of the questions has been whether to take a specialist or generic approach, and related to this has been the need to mesh together long-term preventive approaches with short-term crisis work. Community and patch-based service delivery has tended to ally itself to a more long-term preventive approach, but it has always struggled to provide the statutory cover that has been increasingly necessary as legislation loads more tasks onto already stretched resources and staff.

The 1983 Mental Health Act brought in the approved social worker. The 1986 Disabled Persons Act brought in some measures, such as independent representation, that were never enacted. The 1989 Children Act placed children firmly at its centre, reinforced the position of the family, and advocated parental responsibilities, at the same time as emphasizing the importance of partnership in looking after children — partnership between parents and Social Services departments, and a partnership between Social Services departments and others.

Following on from this, the National Health Service and Community Care Act 1990 has the same sort of philosophical underpinning. Service users are central to the legislation as are their relatives/carers/families. Social Services are asked to work in partnership with users and carers and all the other agencies that are involved in community care.

But Social Services are also asked to become purchasers rather than providers of services. Provision of service will be increasingly carried out by agencies from the independent sector.

If all this runs its natural course, it is, without doubt, "goodbye" to Social Services departments as we have come to know them.

The purchasing authority of local government for social care in the next century may be part of central personnel or located elsewhere in the chief executive's department. It will be a unit made up of senior managers, planners, communication staff, monitoring and inspecting staff. It will be their business to purchase services for those who need them, within budgets determined largely by the government.

The provider units will be the workplace for most of today's Social Services staff.

Service users and carers/relatives are quite rightly being given a greater say in how services should be provided. This will mean more imaginative, less professionally oriented services. But there is a fear, which users and carers themselves share, that resources will not be available to meet the needs.

The hope lies with the increased power of those who use services and their carers/families, as well as with the staff across all agencies who are really trying to break down institutional and professional barriers to work together.

The consultant's task will be to energize people to cope with the changes and come through them fighting, together, for better services for all who need them.

CHAPTER FOUR

"You have an interesting way of seeing things": consulting within a Social Services department

Robin Burgess
Systemic Consultant, currently Training Manager
in a West London Social Services Department.

[In this case study, sensitive and elegant use is made of the role of internal consultant in a Social Services department. It shows how informal conversations with an individual can become a vehicle for systemic consultancy, with the nine stages of the model (Diagram 1) collapsed into a briefer and perhaps more complex process.

Robin Burgess's broad understanding of the beliefs of the organization within which he is working allowed him to position himself strategically so as to maximize his effectiveness. In this case, the power issues around a formal declaration of himself as different from his peers via the label of consultant led him instead to position himself as a helpful colleague with an "interesting way of seeing things".

This case study is also a powerful illustration of an observing system in which it was possible to maintain the curiosity of the consultee.

In this connection, we note that Robin also sought consultancy for himself to maintain this sense of a "just noticeable difference". Within his broad framework of understanding about the organization as a whole, Robin developed a nest of further hypotheses, including those about his own role as a person with interesting ideas/consultant. What is most impressive here is his lightness of touch! — Eds.]

SCOUTING: A FRAMEWORK FOR OPERATING

A belief that underpins this case study is that one's effectiveness as a consultant to colleagues within a Social Services department is inversely proportional to one's use of the label "consultant".

There are of course other important variables to being effective; but in fourteen years of family therapy and systemic practice in this environment, I have found it has rarely enhanced my manoeuvrability as consultant within a Social Services department to promote a formal image of consultancy.

One meaning of consultancy

The hypothesis that I have developed is that social workers carry so broad and blurred a remit that their sense of professional confidence and identity is rarely robust in the face of consistent knocks. This has the effect of sensitizing them to anything that might seem to undermine autonomous competence.

Social workers customarily use a direct supervisor, who is often so closely responsible for the casework that her or his creative thinking is greatly inhibited. Yet loyalty and possessiveness in this relationship often inhibit use of wider networks.

Informal support is frequently sought from social worker peers, which does not jeopardize a sense of competence or professional autonomy. However, there is considerable shyness of formal consultancy within the organization.

This culture is carried into management, where despite an informal image, there is an acute sensitivity to hierarchy. It can be very difficult for a manager to acknowledge being advantaged by the insight of a junior or even a peer.

40

Formal consultancy is perceived to imply a one-down position, and hence it is usually only sought from an outsider or on rare occasions from superiors. There is, in my experience, therefore, little response to offers of consultancy. On the other hand, there is considerable response to being seen to be someone who has an interesting way of seeing things during informal chats.

An informal framework such as this carries pitfalls as to effective contract negotiation, and to scope of intervention. In the case study that follows I explore this further.

I hesitate to identify a model that most informs my approach to consultancy, as to do so plays into the myth that we operate within rigidly defined constructs. Like most family therapists who have developed wider consultation frameworks, my approach is built on integrating what "fits" for me from a range of models and disciplines.

Nevertheless, the foundation on which I have built is derived from a Milan systemic training. The use of questioning guided by disposable hypotheses; the connections between beliefs, relationships, and behaviour; managing meaning; reframing and redescription; making new connections for the consultee which need not necessarily be within the consultant's awareness, but enable change—all these play a part in my consultancy toolkit (informal and not so informal).

ENTRY AND CONTRACTING

I have been training manager in a Social Services department for three years. For nearly two years I *scouted* formal opportunities to apply my consultancy skills internally, with little success. Gradually, informal consultees increasingly asked for opportunities to talk something over. The process of *entry* was reversed, as it was they who drew me into their system.

On one such occasion, Angela, (who had been head-hunted to take over a new developmental team considered crucial to the department's vision), identified an informal *contract* by her request to talk over a problem with: "This is more as a friend than a colleague." This blurred boundaries for me at one level, constraining my position as consultant. At another level, I was provided with a basis of trust and confidence. The challenge for me, which made me select this case study, was to maintain an awareness of my tendency to be drawn into a coalition. My response was to feedback a more neutral frame: "I'm happy to listen, my thoughts may or may not be what you are looking for."

DATA GATHERING

I employed "key-word questions" to keep the data gathering focused on process. An advantage of this form of question for intervening into content narrative is that because the question carries actual words used by the consultee, it enables a shift towards process without a sense of being interrupted. The consultee whom it enables still feels listened to and valued. For example, after much detail of who said and did what:

ANGELA: "— and she ignored my request to fill in a desk diary of her movements, and no one else has . . ."

ME: "Does she ignore [a key word] anyone else's requests?"

An advantage for the internal consultant, which balances the struggle for neutrality, is detailed knowledge of the culture and the behaviour and beliefs of key players. Angela's dilemma was the insubordination of a member of her team. She had tried so hard to engage this quiet and previously cooperative woman who had been moved into her team, but she was consistently met with firm, silent resistance. Angela was at the end of her tether and was convinced she was dealing with a personality problem. I resisted a pull to stand with Angela and maintain the staff member as the problem; I stayed with a curiosity to identify a systemic meaning for what was happening.

I was aware of the culture constraining an avoidance of open conflict in the department, but I also carry a belief that personalized conflict in organizations is the conveniently "stuck" alternative to change elsewhere. I questioned further about the previous management structure and raised for Angela an awareness that this staff member was previously supervised by Angela's own boss, who asked Angela to take her into her recently created team. This had not involved consultation with the staff member. Furthermore, because of the nature of her work, Angela's boss continued to commission work directly from this staff member without involving Angela.

I was beginning to form a hypothesis, which I needed to refine, and I left Angela at the end of the first meeting with a *reframe*. I suggested that her staff member might not be so much a personality problem, as someone who had experienced being devalued and demoted by her previous boss. However, because she still had an investment in maintaining the direct access still offered by this senior manager, she focused her anger over this experience into her relationship with Angela, her new and less senior boss.

The opportunity to talk about this stressful situation and being offered a different meaning for what was happening meant that Angela felt interested and unburdened. However, although I suggested she drop by again to talk further, the informal nature of our "contract" meant that I would wait until Angela felt enough of a crisis to call in again.

DIAGNOSIS AND PLANNING

I developed my systemic understanding of what was happening by focusing on what the *beliefs* underpinning the behaviour of the participants might be, rather than on their behaviour in itself.

Angela's boss, also a woman, was, I knew, committed to the success of Angela's team. She had also had a long working relationship with Angela's staff member, supervising her occasionally and commissioning her to do work directly for her. This she found difficult to relinquish. I think that she was unaware of how undermining to Angela this was, despite its blatancy. I assumed her investment blinded her to its effects.

I knew the staff member to be sensible and reasonable in other contexts. In her relationship with Angela, I perceived her to experience Angela as a threat to the virtual autonomy she had previously experienced, and to be locked into a battle to keep control over her job and her relationship with her ex-boss.

When Angela returned I would recommend that she examine how she could make her boss aware of how she was experiencing being undermined in her efforts to manage her new subordinate. I would also explore with her how she might set clear boundaries and sanctions on important areas of her management of her subordinate, once she had gained her boss's support. Both would have to be achieved in a way that avoided blame and further conflict of personalities. The framework would need to be the effective achievement of shared goals.

INTERVENTION

"You won't believe what she's done — she's baulked authority over taking flexi-time, totally disregarding proper authorization. Have you got a few minutes?" Angela was livid, and although I could not meet her then and there, we arranged a time soon after.

It was not easy to disengage her from a blaming, conflictual frame. In it she was bound to intensify misunderstanding, but she was equally paralysed from acting effectively as a manager because she did not feel she could win.

I took a different tack to depersonalize the conflict, using the analogy of battle for control between parent and child, particularly an adolescent. The reframe of a testing-out to see whether Angela could actually hold effective boundaries in the context of autonomy/dependence, and of Angela's being undermined by the senior "parent", prepared the way for Angela to realize that she could not establish a change with her staff member without gaining the support and backing of her boss.

Having all the experience of a black woman who has achieved on the management ladder, Angela was very effective at translating the above framework into an assertive, non-blaming message to her boss. She would ask her to help sort this out by going through, not around Angela, if she needed work from Angela's staff. Not unexpectedly, the response was positive and supportive.

Once she was convinced of support from above, the disempowerment in relation to her supervisee was lessened. The challenge for Angela had been to develop a new approach, although one that she was less confident in: being direct, rather than engaging by being supportive. I reframed the disregard for her authority over taking flexi-time as a message that the relationship was so unsafe for the staff member that she was now exposing her insubordination in a way that invited and facilitated clear boundary setting. It was a gift and an opportunity, rather than just a threat.

EVALUATION

Angela was effective enough in establishing boundaries without getting stuck in personalized conflict. However, she was constrained by the strong organizational culture of avoiding overt conflict and directive management. Understanding this perspective, however, enabled her not to take upon herself full responsibility for feeling de-skilled in this situation, when she was normally so competent.

Had I not been internal to the organization and experienced my own battles with the same culture (I used systemic consultancy from colleagues both internal and external to my department), I might have needed a lot longer to understand this context to Angela's dilemma. So I was both consultant and consultee in the organization. Angela's own verdict: "You have an interesting way of seeing things. It's very helpful talking to you."

CONCLUDING THE CONSULTANCY

Like *entry*, *withdrawal* from this informal consultation system was initiated by the consultee. Despite the frame of friendship, chosen to ensure informality and a greater sense of control by the consultee, I did not feel unduly constrained. I am now more confident to negotiate a little more structure for "my interesting way of seeing things".

Other colleagues have become curious when they have been in crisis. The most enduring feedback is about being a good listener. Providing reframes and questions that catalyse new connections and options is experienced less consciously. Such skills may also be somewhat threatening, compared to being a good listener. In an environment in which all too many people want to take others' problems and solve them for them, being heard may also be the difference that makes a difference.

One notable element of this case study is that the interactions with the consultee occurred only at times when she experienced crisis. At one level, she required the validation of being heard; at another, she needed a difference that could unstick being stuck. Crisis is always a favourable context for facilitating change.

FURTHER REFLECTIONS

The Social Services are not the only organizations where the culture does not encourage formal use of colleagues as consultants. It is more likely to be the case wherever role expectations are blurred. In multi-disciplinary settings, I have noticed that colleagues use one another more freely for consultancy though usually across disciplines.

The climate is, however, changing in the Social Services. Through the influences of family therapy (where co-working, teamwork, and consultation are often in-built), and of changes in social work training itself, there is a growing tolerance to one's practice being scrutinized.

Diploma in Social Work students are required to have some live supervision on their practice placements. Their practice teachers, in their turn, are required to provide evidence of live observation in order to be accredited. These requirements can only be the vanguard of a culture change in Social Services to facilitate the use of colleagues as consultants.

Simply put, the process of using another person's ideas to achieve an observer position from which to achieve new meaning in complexity or stuckness is a prerequisite to survival in the numerous contradictions of current Social Services. My perspective is, to use the current jargon, from both positions of "purchaser and provider".

CHAPTER FIVE

Internal consultancy to group leaders running a sex offenders group

Martin Wrench
Senior Social Worker in a Regional Forensic Psychiatry Team

[This case study is more formal than the previous example, involving a marketing process and a formal request for consultancy. It is written by someone who would not call himself a systemic consultant, but it well illustrates the recursive relationships between the wider organization of a prison and the groups and individuals within it; and how these, in turn, affect dealings between one organization — the prison service — and another — the NHS.

Martin Wrench's understanding of the systemic issues around the prison system in general and sex offending in particular helped to inform his consultancy about the therapeutic process in groups for sex offenders; the unfolding relationships in the groups themselves in turn helped him to elaborate the systemic picture. The theme is the degree of constraining and/or autonomy possible in working with sex offenders.

This case study is also an excellent example of inter-agency collaboration and of the value of internal and external consultants working together, particularly within the closed system of a prison. In this case, one of the group leaders was internal to the prison system, whereas the other was part of the NHS. The consultant was also part of the NHS, but of a different discipline from the group leader. This maximized the possibilities of being able to develop different perspectives and a creative integration between what could have been an unhelpful polarity between therapy (represented by the NHS) and punishment (represented by the prison system).

As Martin Wrench himself points out, the success of the "pioneer groups" led to them being owned and run by the prison system itself. The possible loss is of the additional perspectives and creative tension provided by inter-agency collaboration. — Eds.]

SCOUTING

I am employed as a senior social worker in a multi-disciplinary team that works with mentally disordered offenders. In the summer of 1991, the senior clinical psychologist in the team asked me if I would be prepared to provide consultancy to her and a male probation officer with whom she was planning to lead a group for sex offenders at the local prison where the probation officer was based. The group, to take place weekly, would have a membership of between six and ten men, all of whom would be serving sentences for sexual offences against children.

I had previously provided consultancy to the psychologist and another psychologist in the team in relation to a group they were running. The fact that this had proved useful to them was one reason why the psychologist approached me regarding the sex offenders group. An additional factor was that I had recently circulated a statement within the department reminding colleagues that I had completed a two-year course on consultancy. The statement emphasized that I would be offering a primarily process consultancy approach, in which the consultant's role is to help the clients form their own diagnosis of a problem and subsequently generate, select, and implement solutions.

I believe the group leaders were further motivated by the wish to discuss the group with someone with relevant expertise who was outside their respective line-management structures. In our department, each discipline is supervised and managed by its most senior representative. I am managed by my social work teamleader and the psychologists are managed by the department's consultant psychologist. I clearly had no management role with respect to the group leaders or the group itself, and it was understood from the beginning that the primary distinction between supervision and consultancy was that the group leaders took full responsibility for the group and for implementing any ideas that developed from the consultancy sessions. I believe the group leaders favoured consultancy over supervision, because it allowed a measure of autonomy and a degree of responsibility that would reduce the sense of being functionaries in a rigid and, by definition, punitive system and would thereby heighten the creative, therapeutic aspect of their roles. Furthermore, to be supervised by one of their managers would have created an asymmetrical relationship; that is, a psychologist or a probation officer would be supervising another discipline. By contrast, in coming to me for consultancy as opposed to supervision, they would be entering a non-hierarchical relationship with someone who worked alongside the psychologist on a day-to-day basis and who came from a discipline closely allied to probation. I could be viewed from this perspective, therefore, as someone who could develop a meta-perspective of the system as a whole.

Interestingly, while not initially aware of this dimension to the request, I felt a strong need from the beginning to adopt a strategic stance that favoured neither one nor the other group leader. From my perspective, this stemmed from my concern that my day-to-day working relationship with the psychologist would bias me in her favour. This concern led me to establish a ground rule in the exploratory period before the group began: that the psychologist and I should not discuss the group outside the consultancy sessions. I considered that while this was, in itself, a sensible boundary, it needed to be made especially clear to prevent any potential splitting between the group leaders resulting from my well-established working relationship with the psychologist. However, my concern actually created a split by reinforcing the notion that the probation officer was external to my organization, whereas, for the purposes of the group and the consultancy, both he and the psychologist could be viewed as members of the same wider system comprised of the department and the prison and probation service.

It is difficult to evaluate what effect my incomplete understanding of the system in the early stages had on the consultancy process, but it would be realistic to consider that it may have limited my effectiveness in helping the leaders understand their respective and joint roles in the system. My strategic stance with regard to the leaders may also have prevented an examination of their differences, including such an obvious difference as the fact that the psychologist was a woman who, together with a male co-leader, was working with an all-male group of sex offenders. This could, I feel, have been even more of an issue for both leaders if the men in the group had offended against adult women as opposed to children of both sexes.

A broader issue affecting the system is that at the time there was no strategy in place relating to the treatment of sex offenders in the prison. However, a group treatment model developed by a Home Office psychologist was soon to be implemented. In the early stages the probation officer and the psychologist experienced direct and indirect challenges from the prison officers which was evidenced by delays in the prisoners being released from the cells and by prison officers interrupting group sessions. Sex offenders are generally a detested section of the prison population and require segregation from the other prisoners for their own safety. Also, the fact that a probation officer and a psychologist — representatives of the less custodial, welfare and treatment aspect of the prison system — were going to provide groups for these men undoubtedly aroused some opposition from more traditional elements in the prison system. Whether the members of the group were aware of the dilemmas posed by the existence of the group is open to question.

ENTRY

I met with the group leaders twice before the group began. The purpose of these preliminary meetings was to determine what the group leaders wanted from the consultancy process and to clarify whether that was consistent with what I was able to offer. We established that they wanted consultancy to assist them in identifying and exploring issues raised by the group process and to help them find solutions to any difficulties. They viewed consultancy as a facilitative as opposed to prescriptive process, and this was very much in keeping with my own perception of the consultant's role.

CONTRACTING

It was agreed in these preliminary sessions that we would meet weekly after each group session at the department where the psychologist and I are based. The reason for meeting almost immediately after the group was partly practical in that it suited our respective work arrangements. Another reason, however, was the group leader's view that it would be particularly useful to discuss the experience of the group and the feelings it generated while they were still fresh. What happened in practice was that they would come to the department from the prison immediately after the group and on arrival would meet together for twenty minutes, prior to the consultancy. This brief meeting enabled them both to gain some initial grasp of the key issues in the session as well as to consider their programme for the following session. Perhaps it also helped the leaders hold on to a notion of a therapeutic process, which might have been difficult in the prison.

It is difficult to ascertain to what extent conducting the consultancy in a health service environment, away from the prison environment in which the group was run, may have affected the consultancy process overall, but it may have served to re-enforce the group leaders' separateness from the prison system and its culture. If the consultancy had occurred in the prison, I would have felt that I was bringing a new perspective into the system; whereas, by providing consultancy at a distance from the institution, my contribution may have been rendered invisible to all but the group leaders and the probation officer's senior, who also worked in the prison.

The consultancy process was to last fifteen months, and during this period the group leaders ran two groups, each of six months' duration. Three members of the first group became members of the second group. Each group session lasted one and a half hours, and the consultancy sessions were of one hour's duration.

DATA GATHERING

At the beginning of each session, the group leaders were invited to state their key concerns following the group session. In the early stages of the group, they were primarily concerned with difficulties they experienced with the prison system. The group sessions were frequently interrupted by prison officers, and there seemed a general unwillingness to accept the group's existence within the institution. This was, perhaps, a reflection of how sex offenders are viewed within the prison system, as well as possible evidence of some distrust and competitiveness towards psychologists and probation officers. The task of sorting out many of these difficulties and the preservation of the group's boundaries within the prison fell to the probation officer, who was more obviously part of the prison service than the psychologist, and he was identified within the group in the early stages as "the fixer". Over the months, we explored similar issues raised by the system and the roles it imposed on the group leaders, and in time the leaders developed strategies for managing their relationship with the institution.

A key issue was how some group members perceived the group leaders as "teachers", authority figures whom they experienced at some level as uncaring and unfeeling. This may have been a reflection of how the programme for the group sessions was structured, as there were specific topics to address in each session which required some didactic input from the group leaders. In other respects, however, the teacher role could be construed as a projection by group members upon the group leaders, which made their role congruent with other prison staff who are, for the most part, authority figures. Additionally, the group members may in the early stages, at least, have felt more comfortable with the group leaders as teachers than as therapists, because the former role would allow the group members to maintain a greater emotional distance from the nature and the effects of their offending. The consultancy sessions provided an opportunity to explore this and other projections by the group onto the group leaders; they also enabled the group leaders to make adjustments in their leadership styles that allowed the group members' feelings opportunity for constructive expression without deflecting from the planned focus of the group sessions. For example, particularly powerful feelings were generated in the group by a video showing victims' reactions to their abuse. The group members expressed anger towards the leaders for exposing them to this material. We were able to explore in the consultancy why their response to the material was so angry and intense, and we developed the view that this response related to their own unresolved victim experiences and their sense of being "victims" of abuse by the group leaders. This sense of victimization was probably heightened by the feeling of abandonment engendered by the group leaders' Christmas break, which followed that particular session. The group leaders were able to make use of what they had learned from the experience when they used the same material in the second group.

Another theme that was explored as the group progressed was the role of different group members. For example, considerable time was devoted to difficulties raised by a verbally aggressive and menacing group member. The feelings aroused in the group leaders by group members was another topic; others included the effect of changes in group membership (e.g. group members being transferred to other prisons) and other major transitions including the ending phases of the two groups.

DIAGNOSIS

We evaluated the consultancy process mid-way through each group's life and at the end of the six-month periods. As well as discussing with the group leaders how they experienced consultancy, I also gave feedback on how I experienced it. Working with sex offenders, even at a comparative distance, can generate powerful feelings and powerful opinions. At times, I had to struggle against an impulse to prescribe particular interventions, and I sometimes experienced irritation with the group leaders for being obtuse and not seeing my point. I shared these feelings with the group leaders as an aid to developing an understanding of processes in the group. This conflict between desires for control and punishment of sexual offenders combined with caring/therapeutic impulses was mirrored by the prison system around sexual offenders. In turn this mirrors the way in which sex offenders can be seen as struggling between a desire for control and a desire for closeness and contact with their victims via sexual abuse.

A major theme throughout the group's life was the way that members' distorted cognitions about abuse manifested themselves in the sessions and affected group processes. Sex offenders frequently justify their offending behaviour by claiming that their victims seduced them or enjoyed the abuse — that is, that they were not exercising control over their victims but that it was a mutual process between adult and child. Ideas of this nature can be challenged by therapists or by other group members, but subtler, less easily challengeable ideas can also be present; for example, there was a tendency for a perverse, distorted hierarchy to establish itself in the group between those who had abused numerous children and those who had, as one member in particular saw it, only abused one girl in the context of a "loving relationship", claiming the caring aspect of the relationship to be paramount. A form of competition arose as to who was the "best" or "worst" abuser. I saw it as my role to enable group leaders to explore their own feelings and value-judgements about what constituted more, or less, harmful offending patterns in a way that allowed them to avoid being drawn into or seduced by the group members' ideas. It was important in this connection to recognize that the group members may have been exploring the nature of the group experience in the prison as well as the nature of their offences. Was the group a controlling/punitive or a caring/therapeutic experience?

EVALUATION

In evaluating the contribution of consultancy to the group, we agreed that, by heightening their understanding of the group process and the wider system, this enabled the leaders to deliver the core programme with greater sophistication and awareness of the needs of the group members than would have otherwise been possible. For example, in subsequent groups, the group leaders planned the showing of the video at a different time and in a different way. Consultation also enabled them to manage prison officers' hostile responses to the group more appropriately, due to their improved understanding of the meaning of the groups in the wider system.

It is difficult to evaluate the effect of the group on the members in terms of changes or reductions in their offending, as many of them have not been released into the community and those who have would have been released only recently.

The majority of group members showed a high level of commitment to the groups, and a high level of group cohesion was attained which allowed the men to keep to tasks and, where appropriate, to challenge and support each other. In subsequent groups, those prisoners amongst the group members with more privileges were allowed to take on the responsibility of ensuring that group members with fewer privileges were allowed out of their cells on time to attend groups. The probation officer and the psychologist both stopped working at the prison shortly after the groups ended, and this made it difficult to assess the impact the group had on the prison. However, shortly afterwards prison officers began running similar groups as part of the Home Office Sex Offenders Programme. Groups for sex offenders have become available to an increasing number of prisoners in the last two years, and the prison system has adjusted constructively to this development.

WITHDRAWAL

The psychologist and I are now planning to co-lead an out-patient group for sex offenders as part of the developing sex offenders service in our department. Our collaboration regarding the prison group clearly played some part in this decision to co-lead a group, but we have yet to discuss the changes in role that the new group will necessitate or any further implications it might have. We are currently negotiating with the probation officer to see whether he also would be willing to participate in our department's sex offender service.

From my experience of consulting to the leaders of the "pioneer groups", it seemed very important that one group leader came from outside the prison system and represented the NHS or caring/therapeutic part of the wider system around sex offenders. It was extremely valuable to be able to see this inside/outside perspective and the different cultures represented by the two group leaders, and to reflect upon the mirroring of conflicting impulses in the sex offender and in the wider system as a whole around sex offending.

It may be that groups led exclusively by prison officers would be less able to make use of working with these themes. The fact that I am now leading sex offender groups in the community with the psychologist group leader will not mean, I hope, that we also lose this extra perspective. It is with this in mind that I am seeking to involve the probation officer in our work.

CHAPTER SIX

Systemic consultancy
to a "care" organization

Peter Hollis
Psychiatrist, Family Therapist, and Group Analyst,
working in South London

[This case study is an excellent example of negotiating a position
from which one can bring about change. The role of psychiatrist
to a children's home proved constraining to addressing relationships in the organization as a whole, which were in turn limiting the
contribution Peter Hollis could make. He carefully describes the
process by which he negotiated a consultancy role, suspending his
role as psychiatrist for a period. This crucially involved the chief
executive of the organization, by appealing to this person's task
of maintaining the cost-effectiveness of the psychiatric input, but
also engaged his participation in the whole process. The emerging
rivalry between the consultants and managers was addressed as
the consultancy unfolded by consistent attention to the way in
which this conflict between management and support/supervision
represented a dilemma that was keeping the organization at a
standstill.

This case study is also fascinating in that it involved not only the
use of a systemic framework, but also the use of skills and techniques associated with this approach. The use of hypothesizing,

circular questioning, system interventions, and reflective discussion is clearly demonstrated. —Eds.]

Organization context

The organization was a children's home, one of several operated by a national charity, with a high degree of autonomy in relation to internal structure and functioning at the local level. The organization's task was to provide, for disturbed children, care and treatment, permanent placement in substitute families, and post-placement support. Many of the children, aged between 2 and 14 years, had had previous placement breakdowns, and most were considered by their local authorities as "difficult to place". Typically, a child would remain resident in the organization for about 18 months, while both treatment was being provided and a permanent placement being prepared. My established role was as a psychiatric consultant with the agreed task to advise and consult with care staff and managers jointly over issues raised by specific children, relating to their diagnosis, care, treatment, placement, etc. My contract was with the chief executive in the local organization, to whom I was directly accountable.

SCOUTING

I decided to offer systemic consultancy after recognizing recurrent patterns in the roles and tasks that staff, including myself, were taking up. These were:

1. Cases were presented by junior staff, often key workers, with strong feelings about the children's needs, who were often in conflict with other care staff who were key workers for other children. This conflict between the individual needs of children (e.g. for attention) versus the needs of the group as a whole (e.g. for control) was often presented for my adjudication.

2. Senior staff tended to dismiss key workers' strong feelings about children impatiently, reminding them about the outside constraints (financial, legal, etc.), presenting these as unalterable. This aroused feelings in the key workers of being under-valued and frustrated in their task of child care.

3. It appeared that I was being used by the system to represent the care staff's concerns to the senior staff, and vice versa. I was being invited to referee their conflict, more direct communication being blocked, it seemed, by the key workers' fear of being accused of incompetence and sacked, and by the senior staff's insensitivity to the demands of the child-care relationship with deprived and damaged children.

From my experience of systemic work with families, I recognized that second-order change in the organization would be necessary if it was to move beyond the redundant patterns of communication that were now established.

Since these redundancies had already been noticed and commented on, both by myself and staff, I felt I was well placed to make the case for a need for them to be specifically addressed, and I also felt that I, with a colleague, could offer to work with staff on this.

My colleague was a woman with social work training, with whom I had worked for several years in another context (child and adolescent mental health), providing systemic and other forms of family therapy. From here on, "we" refers to the colleague and myself together.

ENTRY

I asked that we meet with the chief executive to discuss this proposal. He agreed and included his deputy in the meeting. I explained my view that recurrent patterns were being shown in the psychiatric sessions, and I suggested that it might be fruitful for the organization to address working relationships more directly. I said that the discussions ostensibly about children were being used repeatedly in attempts to address the organizational issues, which I then outlined, but that progress on them was blocked since the remit of psychiatric sessions was primarily child focused. The deputy agreed with this view of the sessions, and the chief executive accepted that it would be helpful to facilitate change. He was interested in change, particularly if, as we suggested, some systemic work might well reduce the ongoing need for psychiatric input, and hence reduce costs. Framed in this way, our offer of systemic work became seen as an investment for the chief executive, and we were able to negotiate payment for my colleague and me to work together after explaining that co-working would be more effective.

CONTRACTING

The chief executive negotiated our payment with his own managers, with our support. We were contracted for six monthly sessions, accountable directly to the chief executive, and paid for out of the organization's training budget held by him. My psychiatric role was suspended, releasing its funding for the project, with the option of renegotiation later (this was never requested).

The national organization funding the children's home supports and values consultancy obtained by its constituent units, but it appeared that a special case had to be made by the chief executive for authorization to use the training budget for systemic rather than child-focused work. My colleague and I hypothesized that the chief executive was also using his own hierarchy outside the organization to share and relieve his own anxiety at the new venture, although this was never made explicit.

We asked for authority from the chief executive to expect that all staff would attend sessions, with arrangements made for child supervision, and we asked the chief executive himself to consider our wish that he too should participate, stressing that this would enhance the value of the consultancy for other staff and also ensure that any changes considered would be more meaningful for the organizations as a whole. He readily agreed to participate once we had assured him that we saw our role, in part, as ensuring that the situation would never become too uncomfortable for any one individual.

The staff were then consulted by the chief executive along the lines that we had discussed with him, and he reported back to us that the staff were keen to proceed and also wanted him to participate.

We saw our task as introducing second-order change in the organization, by expanding the systemic understanding of the context of work for the staff, in order to enable them to appreciate the possibility of, and options for, change. To carry out this task, we needed a mandate from both staff and management to conduct a series of sessions asking questions of the whole staff group.

In relation to the chief executive, we were hired by him to provide a time-limited service, which, he felt, after discussion with us, his staff, and his superiors, would be valuable to the organization for which he had responsibility and accountability, and constituted a good investment of time and money already allocated for training within the organization.

DATA GATHERING/ DIAGNOSIS/INTERVENTION

We agreed that it was necessary to think in terms of tasks, roles, and organization structure rather than behaviours, relationships, and beliefs. We hypothesized that task, role, and structure might show recursive links, which might be a description of the process of organizations managing change while maintaining continuity over time. We saw the opportunity to use circular questioning aimed at articulating the links between task, role, and structure in a way analogous to their use in family therapy to explore the links between behaviour, relationships, and beliefs in families, with the intention of facilitating change.

We adopted a second-order cybernetic perspective, thinking about recursive links between the consultees, the organization as a whole, and us the consultants, again couched in terms of task, role, and structure. What tasks had we agreed to perform, how would we negotiate roles with others in order to carry out the tasks, and what structure would this create both in our own consultant subsystem and in the larger system? We saw the intention to be neutral towards change, both in pace and direction, as a crucial element of a second-order approach allowing us to be more responsive to feedback from the rest of the system.

To operate this, we loosely adopted the five-part session format of hypothesizing, questioning, review, message, and afterthoughts.

Our initial hypothesis was that the organization showed a hierarchical structure, with each role having tasks of accountability upwards and responsibility downwards; but that this structure was probably internally inconsistent, giving individuals or sub-systems contradictory information about roles and tasks.

Session One: summary

Thirty staff, including the chief executive, were interviewed by us for a total of two hours to draw out the different beliefs about the organizational structure. Our aim was to persist with questions about who was accountable to whom, and who was responsible for whom or what, until a degree of consensus was reached. At the end of the session, we were able to draw up the organizational structure in diagram form on a large flipchart, together with various points that appeared important to the group. These included :

1. the isolation of the chief executive in his role;
2. distortions of the management hierarchy for supervision purposes;
3. inversion of the hierarchy when seen from the point of view of the child.

Session Two

Hypothesizing

"Management" and "Supervision" were being seen as different tasks implying different roles and different organizational structures. They seem to be conflictual but inseparable. We decided to question around beliefs on the differences between "Management" and "Supervision" with the aim then of exploring the relationship between them.

Questioning

We presented ourselves as interested in any difference that anyone in the staff group could identify between these two tasks as carried out in the organization, drawing directly from their own personal experience.

We wrote up the feedback from the group on a large flipchart for all to see, and the differences existing within the organization were summarized as:

"Management"	"Supervision"
Finance-centred	Child-centred
Being told what to do	Being shown how to do it
Controlling	Understanding
Not listening/unhearing	Being listened to
Frustrating	Satisfying

The care staff in the group then spontaneously expressed much criticism with the management role of senior staff in the organization, and many expressed a demand for more supervision from them. At this point, my colleague and I took a break.

Review

We hypothesized that a problem had been identified by some members of the group which seemed to be that they felt there was too much management and not enough supervision. We thought that the balance between management and supervision was controlled by the various roles and structures in the organization, and decided to explore these with future questions around the consequences for roles and organizational structures if the supervision task were to become more frequent or important in some other way.

Questioning

These questions, addressed to the group as a whole, generated expressions of anger and anxiety. Two beliefs emerged: firstly, that if supervision became more frequent, then activity in the organization would become more poorly coordinated (this view was held mainly by the managers); and, secondly, that the consultancy process itself had become confused and confusing (this view was held more generally by care staff).

Review

We had been surprised by the strong feelings expressed and the criticism of us as consultants. We hypothesized that since the group was quite large (about 30 in number) and, in this context, had no imposed structure, these two factors might be allowing the staff to express strong feelings. We thought that the attack on our role was in part an avoidance of the conflict between care staff and managers, which had become translocated onto us and took the form of confrontation now between care staff and consultants — a kind of "management transference". We decided to concentrate on the dilemmas in the organization, and see whether the confrontation with us as consultants could be modified or resolved by doing this. We hypothesized that there was a fear of a lack of management in the organization, and we composed a message.

> "That the whole staff group was in a dilemma. If the senior staff were to supervise more, especially providing the listening component that the care staff had specified would reduce their frustration, then there might be a worry at all levels in the organization. This worry would be that management might not be carried out as it was at present, perhaps resulting in a period of confusion."

The group responded with much frustration, claiming that the message was not helpful and was incomprehensible. Some members went on to criticize our leadership of the sessions, requesting action techniques such as role play.

Afterthoughts

We felt that our message had aroused strong feelings, and therefore had probably been meaningful to the staff, but the nature of this was hard to judge. We felt we were being seen increasingly by many in the group as alternative managers who were failing to manage the consultancy successfully. We felt we had, to some extent, been placed in a dilemma by the staff group, in that if our consultancy was successful, this might demonstrate that the present management of the organization was ineffective in comparison with us, whereas, if the consultation was not successful, this might be construed as showing that the organization was not capable of change. We were also impressed by the strength of feelings consistently demonstrated in this session and thought that it might be helpful to introduce some structure into the group during the consultancy sessions themselves, in order that individuals might be better able to manage and reflect on the feelings aroused in them.

We thought that the request for role play was at one level a good idea in terms of managing anxieties within the group, and that it might also be an expression of a wish to have conflicts and inconsistencies within the organization demonstrated in a clearer manner; but we were concerned not to be organized by the process into behaving as replacement or substitute managers within the organization. It seemed to us that the beliefs in the organization, and the way these were manifest in the structure, meant that it was difficult to provide both better management and better supervision, since these activities were, to some extent, in conflict. We thought that, having pointed out this dilemma in our message, we were being organized to some extent by the group into a more management-type role by providing greater structure and leadership during the consultancy sessions. We decided to organize a role play, as requested, but insisted that the staff self-select themselves into the different groups in the role play: we saw this as a compromise that would allow us to manage the session, provide a framework to contain anxieties, allow a degree of individual freedom of action, and continue to work on the organizational issues.

Session Three: summary

We carried out a role play using two groups, designated "care staff" and "management", with the task of discussing funding for a new project. In the feedback after the role play, the chief executive's difficult role was acknowledged, as was the need for a structure for organizational decision-making. The group appreciated the role play, especially the opportunity for individuals to experience unaccustomed roles, and further action techniques were requested.

Session Four: summary

We decided to continue with role play, introducing the "supervision" element by having three self-selecting groups, with basically the same task of discussing the funding for a new project. The feedback from this role play highlighted the difficult position of "middle management" in the organization, with pressure from both sides. The group again ended this session criticizing our consultancy as confusing, directionless, frustrating, irrelevant, and incomplete, which we felt represented another attack by care staff on their own management diverted on to us. We gave a message in which "we observed that the care staff were quite open in their criticism and demands of us as consultants, whereas perhaps they felt it best to be less forceful with their managers, both in role and in reality, because they might wish to protect their managers from feeling guilty at having to turn down good suggestions". This message acted both as a summary of the themes in the last two sessions and also addressed the dilemma we felt existed in the organization. We felt also that the group was also expressing a wish for us to change our method of working, and, again, we felt we had been placed in a dilemma about the extent to which we should manage the sessions actively by devising tasks rather than merely asking questions, with the concern that this might be seen to imply criticism of the existing management within the organization. We decided to continue role plays but give detailed instructions about tasks specifically focused on proposals for change.

Session Five: summary

Three self-selected role-play groups — "management", "care staff", and "supervisors" — worked separately on proposals for change which were then brought back to a plenary session and written up on the flipchart. We ended this session with an injunction that these suggestions were not to be acted upon, but asked that each group think what it might need to do to enable other groups to behave differently, and what sacrifices this might entail. The proposals for change and this injunction were subsequently typed and sent to each staff member as a permanent record of the consultancy, which was nearly at an end. The group appreciated this session, although the members appeared rather perplexed by the final injunction, which we felt was appropriate.

Final session: summary

We hoped to get general feedback on the issues that had been covered and those that still needed attention within the organization, as well as specific feedback from the last session. After a slow start, ideas were expressed about communication being blocked within the organization, and one of the middle managers proposed a role-play exercise on this subject, which we asked him to organize. We subsequently organized a role play designed to get feedback on the consultation as a whole.

EVALUATION

Six months later, we met with the large group, at our request, to hear views on the situation in the organization.

The chief executive had redesignated himself as project manager rather than project leader, and no longer shared his office with his deputy. His door was, however, seen as ajar, rather than firmly shut as in the past. The home-finding deputy-leader post was abolished, and the home-finding posts, selection, and appointment were brought more under the control of the chief executive.

Staff reported feeling happier and more optimistic at work, but the fear of dismissal remained, fuelled by continuing uncertainty among care staff about their job descriptions and the conditions of employment. We commented on the staff's lack of curiosity about this, suggesting that perhaps they felt it was solely a management responsibility to know about these issues.

Supervision sessions had become more frequent and regular and clearly designated as such, with the conscious attempt to suspend the normal management hierarchy during supervision. However, it was felt that supervision necessarily exposed uncertainties and inadequacies in junior staff to their managers, increasing the fear of dismissal and thereby inhibiting the supervision process. An uneasy tension continued to exist around supervision within a managerial context. The chief executive and his deputies had to some extent resolved this by providing "teaching", which was viewed as a helpful compromise between management and supervision.

CONCLUSIONS

The consultation had a good outcome: there were structural changes in the organization, mood changes for the staff, and a greater awareness of remaining difficulties and contradictions.

Three aspects of the internal consultancy role seemed important in this case study. First, the initial work in the organization by myself in a different role allowed the redundancies in the patterns of communication in the organization to become very apparent, both to myself and to all the staff members. It was, therefore, easy to reach an agreement that there appeared to be a difficulty in the way the organization, myself included, was functioning, and the proposal to address these difficulties more directly was readily accepted. Second, having already worked in the organization, I had gained a measure of trust and credibility from the staff, specifically that they felt I understood the particular dilemmas that their tough work (care of disturbed children) generated. Third, it seemed important to draw a definite boundary around my original role as psychiatric consultant in order to establish a mandate to work in a different way: asking different questions as a systemic consultant to the organization as a whole. It did not seem possible either to myself, my colleague, or the other staff that I could continue in both roles simultaneously, and indeed this did not seem desirable and would have been extremely confusing for all concerned.

The method of hypothesizing, questioning, review, and delivering the message can be practical with 30 people in the initial stages, and the clarification of beliefs about the organizational structure was, in itself, considered helpful by many staff.

Additional techniques were needed later after hypothetical questions about possible change had generated large amounts of anxiety. The use of self-selecting role-play groups allowed us to manage the anxiety and facilitate further work and, in addition, enabled individual staff to experience the organization from another role, which also helps to generate systemic understanding for the individual. The role-plays had a function similar to tasks given to families between sessions, by providing a framework for exploration of conflicts, contradictions, and dilemmas without suggesting specific solutions.

The feedback, both cognitive and affective, generated by our questions was used by us to develop other questions and other interventions. The high level of anxiety called for a managerial response from us as consultants and leaders of the session, and we were able to provide an experience of clear management with a facilitative intent. We developed a facilitating session-management style.

The later role plays took a triangular form, in having two polarized groups, and one neutral group, with the latter taking the role of clarifying but not resolving the conflict. This is similar to the "triangles" technique used with individuals in business consultation and suggests a possible application of this interesting technique in a group context.

The effect on the consultancy of "care" being the organization's task is interesting. Child care is interactional, requiring flexibility of staff roles and behaviour, leading to anxiety, uncertainty, and increasing demands for supervision and/or management. The primary task of child care involves a tension between its facilitating and controlling aspects, which was mirrored in the organization.

In summary, the overall model of hypothesizing, questioning, and review can be useful in consultation to a medium-sized staff group, with the addition of tasks within sessions to both manage and explore anxieties about change. These tasks in themselves can promote systemic work in a similar way to tasks given to families between sessions.

PART THREE

INTERNAL CONSULTANCY
IN THE NHS

Introduction

Bernard Kat
Director of Psychology Services, North Durham

In 1983, Sir Roy Griffiths and his colleagues said of the NHS,

> ... the lack of a general management process means that it is extremely difficult to achieve change. To the outsider, it appears that when change of any kind is required, the NHS is so structured as to resemble a "mobile", designed to move with any breath of air, but which in fact never changes its position and gives no clear indication of direction.

So far as the NHS is concerned, the concept of general management, incorporating the personal responsibility of managers, was the first cultural change leading to increased opportunities for internal consultancy.

The focus on the individual manager creates a critical process of the manager developing an individual cognitive model of the change process, based on a realistic picture of the current situation, a vision of the desired future, and an awareness of actions that will create the desired transition. The degree to which this can happen depends on the strength and abilities of individual managers and their skill in harnessing the best efforts of their staff.

General management was also a universal and centrally imposed change, an example of new and untried systems with internal contradictions being applied in the public sector.

This is the framework within which one must see the second great cultural change, the separation of purchase and provision, foreshadowed in the 2nd Griffiths report on community care. Whereas general management introduced personal responsibility and budgetary responsibilities which make internal consultancy relevant, the purchaser/provider split and the problems of implementing it have revealed key aspects of health and social care systems in a new way. They are not just about services and service provision. To make sense of what is going on, one has to appeal to concepts of system, power, culture, and uncertainty.

More specifically, there is a rhetoric from the Government which specifies ends but appears to leave discretion over means. But the ends are not "pure" in the sense of being about health and social care. They are also about the management of power, especially limiting the financial consequences of medical and local authority autonomy in the context of public demand for services. The chosen means of change are ideology and culture; "managers must have the right to manage" in a task culture; provider competition (imaginary rather than real) operating at many different levels within the systems; multiple ill-defined purchasing functions; uncertainty expressed in "endless reorganization"; and tension about the manageability of the work of professionals and "street-level bureaucrats".

This is hard on everyone because there is no fund of knowledge to which one can appeal to find out what is the right thing to do, or even any simple way of making sense of the situation in which one finds oneself as an NHS worker. The construction of meaning, purpose, and objectives within potentially transient groupings of organizations could become a major industry!

CHAPTER SEVEN

Closing the gap:
consulting in a General Practice

Emilia Dowling
Consultant Clinical Psychologist,
Child and Family Department, Tavistock Clinic, London

[This case study describes the process of negotiating and undertaking long-term consultancy within a General Practice. Instead of going into the practice as a clinical psychologist to see individual patients, the consultant managed to negotiate a wider brief on the initial basis of a teaching/consultancy role. This seemed the most effective position to take, bearing in mind the GP's needs and expectations of the institution where the consultant was based and the relationship with other disciplines in the practice. However, although the consultant/consultee relationship began as a hierarchical one, with the consultee wishing to learn from the consultant, the relationship became a partnership of equals, with both consultants and consultee learning from the process. This is well illustrated by the fact that the consultants and the GP wrote a joint article describing this co-evolutionary approach. At the same time, the consultant was aware of the dangers of becoming too comfortable in this partnership in that it might be difficult to maintain a sense of difference. The use of circular questioning in this connection proved most useful. The evaluation of the consultancy shows that it had a profound effect on the way the GP functioned, both with patients and in her training role. — Eds.]

Background

T
he aim of this chapter is to describe the process of consultancy to a general practitioner in Hampstead Health Authority.

The focus here is on some useful concepts in consultancy and their application to the particular context of the General Practice. A systemic approach is particularly relevant in consulting to a GP as it must, of necessity, involve the wider context in which he or she operates, the professionals who relate to the practice, the individual clients and their families, and the network that GPs have to relate to in order to provide primary care to their patients.

In attempting to draw some principles from this consultancy experience, the following notions are considered:

1 *The nature of the request*

   How does it come about?

   Ways of responding:
   (a) things to bear in mind;
   (b) mandate;
   (c) sanction from others;
   (d) clarifying the brief;
   (e) defining the boundaries.

2. *The contract*

   Understanding the beliefs of the organization – how do others in the practice view the consultancy.

   Negotiating:
   (a) the role;
   (b) the task;
   (c) the boundaries.

3. *The process of the consultancy*

Development of the working relationship.

The acquaintance stage.

The mid-life stage.

Ending.

4. *The wider context*

SCOUTING

This request for consultancy came about as part of a locally organized scheme to offer psychological services to General Practices. A psychologist in the District circulated a questionnaire to GPs, exploring whether they would welcome and benefit from the presence of a psychologist in their General Practice. She then circulated to all the psychologists in the District the information about the GPs wishing for such a service. In the context of the Child and Family Department of the Tavistock Clinic, a colleague psychologist, Valery Golding, and myself decided to respond to the request from one practitioner who seemed to be interested in children and families, particularly in relation to family work.

The general understanding about psychologists in General Practice has been that the psychologist has represented "an extra pair of hands", another professional available in the practice to take on cases, particularly those for whom no apparent organic cause is found. Experience from professionals in the field suggests that psychologists are often in the Practice seeing patients but with little or no contact with the GPs themselves. When considering responding to this request, my colleague and I thought very carefully about offering a consultative way of working as opposed to becoming that "extra pair of hands" in the surgery. For this purpose, we arranged an initial exploratory meeting with the GP. In the course of this meeting we discovered that the practice was staffed by a single-handed GP and a practice manager. The practice was resourced by a community psychiatric nurse, who saw adult patients in their homes mainly, and a health visitor, who ran a baby clinic in the practice. The GP also coordinated and ran a very efficient team who dealt with the terminally ill patients. She enjoyed links and good relationships with a variety of professionals in the local community, ranging from hospital consultants to primary-care workers. She saw her role in a very broad way, which included her involvement with schools, home visits, and a general understanding of the psychological factors affecting physical illness.

ENTRY

At our first meeting, it became apparent that this GP was extremely sensitive to the psychological factors and was well versed in these matters. She expressed particular interest in family therapy and wished to gain an understanding of the systemic forces affecting individuals' problems. We suggested that a way we might consider working would be not just taking cases but thinking with her about the case and helping her to go forward in her interventions with those involved. We also suggested that we might do some family work with her when, after discussion, it seemed appropriate. For the purpose of this chapter, I concentrate on describing the consultative process to the GP rather than the joint work with clients.

As I understand it, the consultative process involves creating the conditions for clients to utilize their inner resources and potential in order (1) to make their own decisions; and (2) to build resources to live with the consequences of those decisions. It is clear to me that in the consultative relationship the responsibility for the decisions and their consequences remains with the consultee. This is an important difference between consulting and training/supervising or managing. I would, of course, emphasize that it is possible and advisable to develop a consultative style of supervision and management, but for the purposes of this chapter I focus on the particular process of the consultative relationship.

CONTRACTING

In terms of accountability and responsibility, it is important to think about who has sanctioned the request and who the consultant is accountable to for the work. In this case we had the sanction from our own organization to spend the time and psychology resources offering such a service to General Practice. This was in line with the general policy of community-based services offered from the Child and Family Department at the Tavistock Clinic. In terms of psychological services in the District, it was part of a scheme whereby various GPs' surgeries would be resourced with a psychological service. A group was formed for psychologists and GPs to meet periodically and to evaluate and review the experience of the work.

We put it to the GP that we should come to her practice for two hours every two weeks, and we would then review the scheme after a year. A particular advantage in operating as a team is that we would be planning to undertake family work, and we thought that the advantages of having a discussion both in front of the client and with the GP would add to and enrich our consultative service to the practice.

DATA GATHERING/DIAGNOSIS/PLANNING

In terms of internal consultancy, the issues arising from this piece of work relate to the fact that being part of Hampstead Health Authority means that the Tavistock Clinic represents a resource for the GPs in the area, as well as for other professionals in the NHS. However, because of the special nature of our institution, its training and consultancy function, and its identity as a national and supra-regional resource, the relationship with the local professionals is one that has to be negotiated, and it is of course a matter of choice for them whether they make use of the Tavistock or not. In this particular case, it was the GP's choice to invite psychologists into the practice, and because of the local relationship it meant that no payment was involved. However, the decision for the involvement was discussed and negotiated, and the GP was, of course, at liberty to terminate the contract if she had so wished. Issues of choice and issues of payment are particularly important in the context of today's NHS. It is necessary to highlight, at this point, that in the recent follow-up discussion with the GP, she commented that maybe to begin with she would not have paid, but after the work was completed and she knew what she had had, she would have paid for it.

Another dimension of the internal consultancy was the GP's view that, although she had some idea about what psychologists and other professionals did at the Tavistock, she was very interested in seeing how psychologists would work in the context of the General Practice. In this respect, the consultee entered into the consultancy in a learning context, hoping to learn from us as consultants. Although she did not make it explicit at the beginning, she commented later that she had hoped for and found flexibility, adaptability, and an interest in fitting in with the context and ethos of the practice whilst retaining the principles that would make it possible to work effectively.

Useful concepts

When thinking about undertaking a new piece of work, it is useful to bear in mind *the beliefs of the organization*. What is the meaning of the consultation happening in and for the organization? What are the expectations, not only of the consultee but of those in the immediate context? In the context of this General Practice, it was important to be clear about the expectations of the practice manager as well as of the other professionals resourcing the surgery. In the course of the work we understood that, for example, the presence of two psychologists in the practice represented a potential threat to the use of the services of the community psychiatric nurse, and it required very skilled managing on the part of the GP to reassure everyone in the practice that she had a very clearly delineated role and boundary for all of them.

Another question is: who will lose or gain by the presence of a consultant? In this case, it could be that the GP might benefit from our presence; on the other hand, other professionals could feel that they might lose out when an extra resource becomes available. We might also ask what the GP had been lacking at this time that led her to ask for extra support from us.

An important notion to bear in mind is that of role. The following questions were helpful in establishing and clarifying our role in the practice.

• In what capacity have you been asked?

- Have you got a mandate to be there?
- Are you there by invitation or by right? In other words, have you a mandate to be there by the nature of your work, or have you been asked specifically to provide a consultative service?
- To whom are you accountable for this work?
- If you were not there, who might be doing what you are being asked to do?

Another useful notion is that of *task*.

- What is the task at hand?
- Is there a big discrepancy between what you have been asked to do and what you think you should do?

The task of the consultancy is to enable your clients/consultees to do their job more effectively. This involves helping the individual or group to be aware of the anxieties and irrational forces that get in the way of the task.

Yet another useful notion in the process of setting up the work is that of *boundary*. Setting the boundaries is very important as a communication. The time boundary suggests that you take the task seriously, that you are reliable, that your consultee deserves respect. The space boundary provides a message of containment of the work: if it is agreed that a particular space is designated for the consultation, there is then an explicit agreement that the work requires a special space and that the physical space is symbolic of the mental space assigned to the task. Having a particular territory — that is, a designated room — to carry on the consultative work, is of extreme importance as a message of continuity.

In our consultancy to the GP, the agreed boundary in terms of time was that we should come in the middle of the day on a Wednesday when surgery had finished. This was a time that the GP had earmarked for development. Therefore she felt justified in creating the space for this work, we did not feel squeezed in between surgeries or other activities, and from the beginning it was recognized that this time and space was worth allocating. The territory used for the consultation was the GP's consulting room.

Although there was another room available, it was used regularly by the community psychiatric nurse. This boundary represented the delineation of function for the different resources to the practice.

It is important to acknowledge, however, the effect this clear setting of boundaries had on us as consultants, and on the other members of the practice. Despite the GP's clarity about who was doing what, there were inevitable anxieties about the effect that our presence would have in terms of overlapping and perhaps conflicting roles. Would the community psychiatric nurse lose his patients to the psychologists? Would it be possible for us to have access to the mothers and babies attending the practice, or were they the "property" of the health visitor?

INTERVENTION

The consultative work was spread over two and a half years, and it could be divided into the following stages.

The acquaintance stage

During the acquaintance stage it was important for the GP and the team of psychologists to get to know each other, their strengths, their skills, and their way of thinking. We had many a discussion about theoretical issues, ways of approaching certain problems, and views about a particular population and a particular illness. During this process a lot was to be learnt and gained, although at times this learning was difficult and painful. We learnt of our ignorance about clients who would not normally come to a psychiatric clinic, which was our work base: patients who come to the General Practice with complaints of a physical nature but wishing to be attended to in a different way. The GP learnt about our ideas concerning the importance of the wider context and the relationships within the system that could affect, perpetuate, and maintain the symptomatic behaviour.

In terms of our evolving working system, it was particularly important to identify both our strengths and our limitations. It was very important to maintain our differences and different perspectives. Only by acknowledging difference would we be able to face it and deal with it with the clients.

The GP wished to learn how to approach problems from a systemic perspective. We often used the tool of the genogram. Through it we were able to elicit the family patterns and the connections between members of a family which perhaps the GP had not seen before, over and above knowing that they were filed under the same surname. It became possible for her to make relationship connections and understand the nature of the symptoms in a different way.

During the consultancy, we tried to concentrate on the process as well as the content of the material discussed. It was important to ask questions such as:

- Why had the GP presented this particular issue in the first place?
- What aspect of her relationship with her patient was most worrying to her? What would be the expected outcome of a different kind of intervention?
- What effect would a decision not to hospitalize a patient have on the rest of the family?

It was also important to ask questions about the effect that particular events had on the GP and on her capacity to manage certain situations. For example, asking questions about the connection between the death of a patient and her way of relating to the relatives provided an opportunity for the GP to explore her own feelings about the deaths of patients and reflect on her patterns of behaviour when confronting death and mourning. This exploration had a powerful effect on us, as it put us in touch with the life-and-death quality of the work in the practice.

These questions, together with the GPs own insights into the situation, often offered the possibility of making links and connections that allowed us to see the situation in a different way, and therefore to develop different ideas about possible interventions. Questions about the effect that a woman's symptoms had on her husband and his reactions to her pains would elicit some understanding about the relationship and the pattern that had evolved around her symptoms. After the consultancy, the GP might choose to meet with the couple, to think about how they could manage the problems, as opposed to just seeing the woman on her own.

The discussion about a 15-year-old girl who was refusing school was broadened from the school-refusing symptoms to the exploration of the wider context in which this girl functioned. Her mother's agoraphobia, her father's drinking difficulties, and the fact that the mother had been recently diagnosed with breast cancer enabled us to develop a hypothesis about how this girl's school-refusing behaviour was more to do with protecting her parents, and in particular her mother, and her anxieties and fears about losing her. Being able to see her difficulty in a different way allowed the GP to intervene with the family and enabled the school staff to understand and respond differently to the problems.

The mid-life stage in the consultation

Most of us will be familiar with that stage in the consultative process where things begin to get a bit cosy. If the consultative relationship has functioned well and developed successfully, it is only too easy to get rather stuck in a comfortable pattern where challenging questions and confronting and facing the more unpleasant and painful aspects of the work becomes more difficult. It is important at that point, particularly if one is enjoying the work, to be able to step outside the relationship and think carefully about evaluating where one has got to — being able to face the possibility of becoming redundant and beginning to think that perhaps the consultative process ought to be coming to an end. If the consultancy has been successful, the consultee would have developed sufficient skills and understanding to pursue and continue the work without the consultant. This is a painful stage, and therefore a review has to be built into the contract so that it is possible to monitor and examine the work from time to time.

In this particular consultancy, it was evident that the GP had been able to use the consultative experience to maximize her understanding and sensitivity to her patients. She had also developed her skills in terms of working with families and, in addition, had been able to use a consultative style of training towards junior doctors who came to the practice. This was a particularly rewarding experience for us, as the GP made it clear that she saw how discussing the issues with the trainee in front of her patient would be beneficial to everyone involved.

EVALUATION

Ending

The final phase of the consultancy involved an evaluation of the work, looking back and reviewing the cases we had thought about together, and the decision to write a paper about our mutual learning and experience. This focused activity allowed us to bring to an end a rewarding and exciting project. What had started out as a teaching/learning relationship evolved into a mutually beneficial process. The process of ending put us in touch with the issues around loss which we needed to work through together in order to enable us to leave the practice with a good experience and for the GP to remain with and to own the skills she had developed.

Our evaluation of the work took place in relation to the objectives set out at the beginning of the project. In the process of evaluating the work, it became apparent that the GP had developed her skills in systemic work with families and therefore felt more able to deal with some of the work in the practice which previously she might have referred elsewhere.

A particularly relevant development for the GP has been the way she consults, when appropriate, with other members of the primary care team in the patient's presence. This has enabled patients to be party to the thinking process by providing feedback to the discussion and taking a more active role in decisions about their health.

This way of working has also had an effect in the training of medical students and nurses in the practice. Patients are now encouraged by the GP to contribute actively to the students' learning by sharing their own knowledge rather than being passive recipients of examination procedures. We witnessed an interesting discussion between a pregnant woman and a medical student regarding changes in her blood pressure. The woman's understanding of what was happening to her was clearly helpful to the student, and her questions provided a focus for the discussion as well as feedback about issues that had not been fully explained.

The wider context

The wider context of this work was the group of psychologists throughout the District who had been providing a similar service to other GPs. Our meetings with these psychologists provided a context within which to examine and discuss our work and review our experience in relation to that of others; it also provided a setting where peer consultancy about each other's issues became possible. As in all groups, issues around rivalry and competition between us had to be managed and dealt with. We needed to be aware of the temptation to see ourselves as doing the work in the "right" way as opposed to a "different" way. However, it was rewarding to see and experience the mutual learning that took place and the gradual evolution towards viewing the work of psychologists in General Practice more in terms of contributing to the work of the GP rather than having to play the "numbers game" by producing a large number of patients seen.

CHAPTER EIGHT

Setting up an ongoing course to enable nurses in an NHS Trust to care for the bereaved

Frank Milton
Chartered Clinical Psychologist,
working in South West Thames Region

[This honest and personal account of entering a system without first having established legitimacy for the work serves as a timely reminder that consultants failing to address this issue do so at some risk. The dilemmas about external versus internal consultancy, the identification of the consultees, and training versus consultancy are clearly described.

The work took place against the background of wider organiza-tional changes including

- changes in organizational structure and management of the units concerned;
- change in the philosophy of care;
- shifts in styles of nurse education.

In the case of the dying and the bereaved, they appear as the proverbial "hot potato" for which the new system has not clearly assigned responsibility. Frank Milton links this difficulty with the stages of the project and the ambivalence about death that characterizes NHS professionals dedicated to preserving life, with little preparation for their "failure" to do so.

What is fascinating is how Frank Milton manages to ride this roller-coaster and produce positive results. His reflections on his own (linear) feelings of anger and despair at various points in the process provided a stimulus to the development of a more systemic view. We are all "wise after the event"! The challenge is to convert this wisdom into meaningful feedback to guide the next stage of the work. This is well illustrated here. — Eds.]

Introduction

For a considerable time I have held the view that psychological concepts and methods are too valuable to be confined only to the arena of "mental health problems", that they could be applied with benefit in other areas, the most obvious being physical medicine.

In addition, enthused by Isabel Menzies-Lyth's paper on "The Functioning of Social Systems as a Defence against Anxiety" (Menzies-Lyth, 1959), it seemed that utilizing psychological understandings with carers could be a fruitful and rewarding exercise.

SCOUTING

Already aware of some of the literature on the psychological aspects of cancer, I decided to approach the local Macmillan Continuing Care Team because they provide a service to terminally ill cancer patients, their relatives, carers, and relevant professionals.

It needs to be said that both the psychology department within which I work and the Macmillan Team are part of a Directly Managed Community Unit, and the nurses from the general hospital with whom we were to become involved were part of an NHS Trust. So whilst being external to the Macmillan Team, I was employed by the same authority, which created some confusion as to whether I was being an external or internal consultant. The Macmillan Team had not expressed any wish for help and or need for change.

These two issues — the confusion over external/internal and my legitimacy for doing the work — were to haunt the project I am about to describe.

What should be mentioned here, and no doubt it will be reiterated later, is that when carrying out the project I did not conceive of it as being consultancy. Consequently, many of the concepts, techniques, and understandings of this approach were not utilized when the work of the project was being done. In view of this, much of what follows is a case of being wise after the event.

Some two or three years ago, the health authority for which I work employed someone, on a short-term contract, to look at the experiences of the recently bereaved in the District. More specifically, the survey was concerned with people who had recently had a relative die in a hospital in the District and how they had been treated by health authority staff. The results of the survey showed a great deal of variation in how the bereaved felt they had been cared for. Some reported being shown considerable kindness and sympathy, whilst others felt they had been treated in a brusque, offhand, and insensitive manner. At the end of the report, the author made some concrete suggestions as to what could be done to improve matters.

ENTRY AND CONTRACTING

It was shortly after the results of the survey had been published, and without knowing of its existence, that I first contacted the Macmillan Team. The Team, all of whom are women, consists of a doctor, a secretary, and three nurses, one of whom manages the Team.

At our initial meeting, I was made aware of the tensions between the doctor, who also works locally as a GP, and the nurse manager. Indeed, their response to my proposal to form a supervision group reflected these tensions, with the doctor being very welcoming of my ideas, although wondering how I had time to do this sort of work when her patients had to wait to see a psychologist, and the nurse being far more guarded about my offer. Indeed, she would

not agree to any involvement on my part until she had cleared it
with her own manager. When the necessary approval was obtained,
it was established that I would meet with the Team for an hour a
week to discuss with them difficulties that they were having with
their patients, and maybe to help the Team look at the way they
functioned. The former was predominantly the nurse manager's
wish, the latter the doctor's.

The views of the other three members of the Team were notice-
ably less audible. I felt that the tensions between the doctor and the
nurse manager were concerned with who really was the boss, the
doctor feeling that her profession gave her that status and yet the
recognized manager was the nurse. It may well be, too, that the
nurse was ambivalent about her position, given the extra responsibility it entailed. The fact that the Macmillan Team were, in part,
worried by my offer, that it would unsettle things, was probably an
indication that they were not doing their work properly and that
they thought I would take sides with either the doctor or the nurse
manager. I suspect too that there was a feeling of relief that maybe
they were going to receive some help and address some of the
problems in the Team.

Regular meetings with the Team were held, and I was presented
with a series of patients whom the various members of the Team
felt to be problematic. Very occasionally, and then only at the doctor's behest, would the Team look at the difficulties besetting it,
which were felt to be of an administrative nature—such as the
problem in keeping records of their work.

Not infrequently, they would make derogatory comments about
male surgeons in the hospital who were interfering in their work,
which gave a good indication of how they saw me and what they
felt about my involvement with them at that time.

DATA GATHERING

When I first started working with the Macmillan Team, they gave
me a copy of the survey on the experiences of the bereaved, and,
from talking with them, it appeared that none of its recommendations had been implemented. I felt that this was something that
needed attending to and that to this end I could use my connection
with the Macmillan Team, who had working links with the medical

and surgical wards. In addition, the composition of the Team would give any work done credibility with senior nurses. It seemed important to target the nurses in the District General Hospital as they were the group of staff with whom the bereaved had the most contact.

My motivation for attending to the non-implementation of the survey was to gain credibility with the Macmillan Team and to engender some legitimacy for my work with them. I felt that this was needed because I was outside the Team and was neither a doctor nor a nurse, so that I did not have the experience of directly attending to the physical ailments of patients. In retrospect this makes sense, as whilst the Team feel that they do "counselling" and "bereavement work", its original raison d'être was the nursing of the terminally ill.

As for the nursing of the terminally ill, and, indeed, the various delays that were experienced during the course of this project, the ideas of Menzies-Lyth are highly relevant. She felt that the work nurses do creates for them a good deal of pain and anxiety, and that these feelings are defended against in an "institutionalized" manner. Carrying out the recommendations of the survey and having nurses look at their feelings in relation to death and bereavement would create anxiety and so had to be avoided or, if this was not possible, postponed. What was also noticeable was the nature of the defence employed — the manic defence. The reason given for delay was that people were too busy and there was so much to be done.

It may be, too, that in the transition of the District General Hospital to a Trust the original report was overlooked. It could have well appeared irrelevant to the task of the hospital at that time, which was the changing of its status.

Also the nursing management may have felt that they lacked the knowledge and skills to put the report into practice, and/or felt that they needed the approval and encouragement of the non-clinical managers of the Trust, which was not forthcoming. There seems to have been an expectation that someone else would do it, perhaps fostered by the fact that the report was compiled by someone who was not a permanent member of the original health authority. I wonder too if the Trust was not waiting for some help in this matter from the Community Unit. Before the General Hospital became a Trust, it and the Community Unit were managed by the same health authority, and the staff of both were colleagues. Maybe in hoping to utilize Community Unit staff the Trust was maintaining links with its past. The move from District General Hospital to NHS Trust could be seen as a kind of death, and in using Community Unit staff the process of mourning would be easier. There would be a greater sense of continuity.

Despite the tensions mentioned earlier, there appeared to be no difficulty in involving two members of the Macmillan Team in the project, in addition to them being part of the supervision group. I simply said it would be a good idea to look at the implementation of the bereavement report, possibly by running a course for nurses, and the Team agreed. I suspect that because I chose to work along-side the two leaders of the Team — the nurse manager and the doctor — my idea was readily accepted, in part because both of them had already toyed with similar ideas and also because my involving them was somehow reinforcing of their authority. It may have been that by taking these two individuals off to work on a joint venture, I was seen as helping to heal the rift between them.

Whether working alongside the two members of the Macmillan Team changed the way they might have perceived me is debatable. What can be said is that from then on there were no further refer-ences to interfering doctors or surgeons or feelings that someone was taking over their work. It would be naive to believe that their transference feelings could have changed so much in such a short time, but there may have been a modification about my working together with these two members of the Team.

DIAGNOSIS AND PLANNING

I discussed my ideas with the Macmillan Team, and we decided on a short course for nurses, consisting of six sessions and entitled "Caring for the Bereaved". At the first meeting with the director of nursing services and her project nurse, we outlined the background to the course and how we envisaged it being run. Arrangements for nurses to have time off work and what time would be most suitable for them were also covered. At a second meeting the doctor and the nurse manager from the team and myself said that we would run the course, and we presented in greater detail what we felt should be included. The director of nursing services and the project nurse welcomed our ideas, and together we drew up a list of specific topics that the course should cover.

It was agreed that the director of nursing services and the project nurse would advertise the course to the nurse managers of the various units (e.g. accident and emergency, surgical, medical), who in turn would put forward nurses they felt would be interested and would benefit from the course. The director of nursing services felt that it was very important that nurses who attended the course should have the support of their nurse managers and should attend every session of what she felt was a much-needed course. The meeting ended with us all agreeing that the course should start in January 1992.

The question could be asked as to how I saw the project of teaching/training as consultancy. The answer is quite simple: at the time of carrying out the project, I did not see it as being consultancy! This probably accounts for the confusions and inconsistencies in the project. It would have been sensible, for instance, to ask who were the consultees and who were the clients. In retrospect, the director of nursing services in the Trust and her project manager were consultees, but the same could also be said of the two members of the Macmillan Team? The nurses who attended the courses were my clients, but, again, could not the same be said of the two members of the Macmillan Team? Related to this is the issue of whose project it was: was it mine alone, or was it mine and the Macmillan Team's? In writing it up, there is a frequent alternation between "I" and "we", which results from the question not being answered.

The confusion as to who were my consultees may have led to a feeling of having to prove myself in the course of the project. As will be seen, great importance was attached to how good the attendance on the course was, and this may have been my measure of saying to the director of nursing services, "Look at what a good course I am running!" It was also a measure that had considerable credibility with the two members of the Macmillan Team, so they and I could say to each other, "What a good course is being run!"

Intervention — the first course

Following our discussion with the director of nursing services and her project nurse, we incorporated the suggested topics into the six

1-hour sessions. The original intention was that the first half of each session should be didactic in nature and the second experiential, where the nurses would have the opportunity to talk over their own relevant experiences. The two members of the Macmillan Team were to lead the first half of each session, and I was to lead the second.

The course members would be asked to evaluate the course during the final session, with a follow-up planned for some three months later.

Results

We have, in fact, run two courses, although I will discuss only the first in detail. A brief discussion of the second course is presented later in the chapter and shows how much we learnt—or otherwise—from running the initial course.

Of the eight who started the course, two were sisters, one was a staff midwife, four were staff nurses, and one was an enrolled nurse.

The titles of the six sessions were as follows:

Session 1   "Introduction. Life Events and Stages of Grief"

Session 2   "Breaking Bad News"

Session 3   "Coping with Relatives' Feelings"

Session 4   "Abnormal Grief"

Session 5   "Tailoring Help to Suit Different Needs"

Session 6   "Looking After Ourselves"

The most obvious changes from my original plan were that only one person would lead each session and that the division of the sessions into didactic and experiential had been lost. The nurse manager of the Macmillan Team ran Sessions 1 and 5, the doctor led Sessions 2 and 4, and I led Sessions 3 and 6.

It was very noticeable that both members of the Macmillan Team devoted practically the entirety of their sessions to formal teaching using video excerpts, overheads, and handouts, all of which were highly appropriate and very well done. Unfortunately, they left little, if any, time for questions/comments from the participants.

I, on the other hand, dispensed entirely with formal teaching and used small and large groups, in which the participants were asked to talk about their experiences relevant to the topic of the session. The aim was for the nurses to reflect on what had happened to them and what, if anything, needed to be different. In most cases, it seemed that they felt that what they were feeling and doing was highly appropriate, and what they needed was to hear approval for that from the other participants and the course leaders. It was very noticeable that the three nurses from the maternity unit were most at ease during group discussions, which reflects the unit's policy of encouraging staff to be open about their feelings when faced with difficult situations such as stillbirths.

Overall attendance at the course was good, though it was noticeable that as it proceeded there were a few absences due to holidays or being on night duty the previous day.

We were left feeling that the course needed to be longer, and we were also concerned that the nurses were leaving the sessions and going directly back to the wards with little time to assimilate what they had experienced. We wondered about improving the attendance and handling the publicity for the course. We felt we should have more control over what the nurses were told about the course and that we should be able to vet all applications.

We then wrote to the director of nursing services summarizing our view on the course and requested another meeting with her.

Review

The director of nursing services reported that from what she had heard the course was a success and we were to be congratulated on our efforts. There was considerable concern on her part about people missing sessions and how this could be avoided in future.

She and the project nurse listened sympathetically to our evaluation and agreed that in future each session should be an hour and a half, though it was felt that the number of sessions should remain the same. They agreed to our having more say in what advance information was sent out and being able to review all application forms. The only difficult moment for me during the meeting was when the doctor from the Macmillan Team said that the valuable part of the course was the opportunity it gave the nurses to talk about their experiences. I managed to bite my lip! Something needed to be said, but for some reason I felt that it was important to maintain a united front in the presence of the director of nursing services and the project nurse. Maybe she noticed this, for towards the end of the meeting she did say how it was I who had enabled the nurses to talk.

Having agreed to changes in the way the course was run, it was decided to begin the next course in October.

Participants' evaluation

The conclusions of the participants' evaluation during the sixth and final session were that everybody found the course useful or very useful and that the most helpful part of the course was the sharing of experiences and discussions. Half the participants felt there should have been more sessions, and all felt that the sessions were too short. Five of the eight nurses felt that the course had changed how they felt about bereavement a little, and a similar number said that it had affected their work to some extent. The questionnaire used did not allow the participants to expand on how attending the course had affected their feelings about bereavement or how their work had changed.

All wanted a follow-up session. As can been seen from below, there was no evaluation by the participants at the follow-up!

Follow-up

Not one of the participants showed up at the follow-up meeting, which left us feeling very angry and disappointed. One of the Team telephoned the director of nursing services, who was apparently extremely annoyed and said that each of the participants would be interviewed about this incident by the project nurse. My own anger about the affair stayed with me for some time, until I realized that the behaviour of the nurses needed to be understood.

As far as I can gather, the nurses have all been seen by the project nurse, but none of what has been discussed has been fed back to us.

The odd comments about annual leave, being on another course, or being on night duty have filtered back. My own thoughts about what had happened are that we made a mistake in not setting the date of the follow-up during the course. Leaving announcing the date until the end of the first six sessions may have broken the continuity of the course for the participants, and the follow-up session would have appeared unrelated to those first sessions.

My other feelings are as follows:

1. The responses to the evaluation questionnaire were too good, as if the participants did not feel safe enough to express any negative feelings about the course. What cannot be put into words will then make itself known in actions. In other words, the nurses were acting out their dissatisfaction with the course.

2. I do wonder, too, about the content of the course—death and bereavement—and what effect that had on the participants. Maybe they wished to avoid further discussion of these difficult matters. Maybe for them there was nothing further to be learnt after the death of the course.

3. There may have been issues relating to what was happening in the Trust itself and with nursing within the Trust of which we had no knowledge.

The second course

For reasons of brevity I will not go into details about the second course but will list the ways it differed from the first.

1. The publicity for the course was compiled by us.

2. The participants had to obtain in writing the agreement of their manager to their attending the course.

3. The course still consisted of six sessions, but each of these was now an hour and a half in length.

4. We vetted and, indeed, selected who of the original applicants should come on the course.

5. The date for the follow-up was given with the original programme.

6. The two members of the Macmillan Team and myself attended the first session, but at subsequent sessions only two of us were present. This means that the cost of the course was reduced.
7. It was noticeable that the two members of the Macmillan Team now allowed time for discussion, utilizing small groups.
8. The non-attendance rate was markedly lower, with only two members being away for one session each.
9. The status of the members was higher than on the first course. On the second course, we had a nurse manager, two sisters, and five staff nurses.
10. All participants attended the follow-up session.

Review

Some time before our second meeting with the director of nursing services and the project nurse, the latter sent to the doctor of the Macmillan Team the first draft of a policy for the NHS Trust on bereavement practices. It cited the original survey on bereavement practices within the Health Authority, as well as Department of Health guidelines and a Nursing Standard on the "Care of the Dying Patient".

Although much of the policy is concerned with procedures such as organ donation and attending to the dead, it does include a section on informing relatives of a death; however, most of this is still procedural, such as arranging for the relatives to view the deceased.

Whatever the omissions in the policy, its appearance is welcome and it may be that our discussions about the course with the director of nursing services and the project nurse have helped it come about.

EVALUATION

This project has involved my working with two systems—the Macmillan Team, and the nurses in a District General Hospital—and, not surprisingly, there are parallels between the two. I will look at the parallels and how they relate to my role as a consultant at the end of this section, but first I need to say something specific about what I feel to be the results of my work with each system.

With regard to the courses for nurses on caring for the bereaved, there was a marked difference between the first and second courses. The former did not appear to be a success, the participants did not seem particularly enthused, there were increasing absentees as the course progressed, and there is no evidence that it changed the way the nurses worked. Nevertheless, the running of the course did give us legitimacy with the director of nursing services and the project nurse, and this, in turn, enabled us to have greater ownership of the second course. In addition, the first course gave the two members of the Macmillan Team the opportunity to see how the sessions could be run differently, and they markedly changed the way they handled the sessions during the course.

This second course did appear to have been very useful: the nurses were more involved in the sessions, and, at follow-up, it was apparent that some of them had learnt a considerable amount. They had contacted other course members about difficulties they had encountered and seemed to be more confident in their work with dying patients and their relatives.

The two members of the Macmillan Team agreed with my evaluation of the course, and, in part, they based this on the greater involvement of the nurses in the second course. All of us seem to have focused on the higher status of the nurses in the latter course, and maybe we equated this with greater ability and hence felt that the second course would be better even before it had started.

One of the major results of the course has been the beneficial effect it has had on my work with the Macmillan Team. Certainly, the course increased my respect for them, and it would appear that it increased their respect for me. It may be that running the course provided an opportunity for some extra reality testing for the doctor and nurse manager, and they were able to see me in a different light. In addition, my helping them run the course gained the legitimacy with them that I wanted. It has been very noticeable that the attitude of the nurse manager has changed considerably, and she is much more involved in the group. Furthermore, she is far more open about expressing her concerns, such as her feelings about what is happening in the Team.

It is possible that the process of the supervision group with the Macmillan Team would have brought about these changes anyway, although colleagues do speak of the benefits of joint working.

Turning now to the similarities in my work with the two systems, the most obvious is the lack of legitimacy that I had with both. The Macmillan Team had not asked for supervision, the director of nursing services had not asked for a course to be run, although both said they were pleased that something had been offered. As I have said, I suggested running the first course on caring for the bereaved to gain credibility with the Macmillan Team for the supervision I was doing with them and also to obtain legitimacy with the director of nursing services for future courses/work with the general hospital nurses.

Having gained credibility, this led to my not letting the Macmillan Team always hide behind patients when what they were bringing were also difficulties with the Team. Consequently, they appear to be more aware of how the difficulties they have with patients are a function of issues within themselves and the Team.

The internal/external confusion was felt most with the Macmillan Team in terms of: "Was I there to help them with patients or the Team?" "Was I there as a Supervisor or a Therapist?" "Could I work alongside them in running courses, or should I remain somewhat distant from them in order to handle better the material they, as a group, were bringing me?" As it turns out, it has been possible to connect up these opposites so they could be seen not as either/or or as in/out, but as to and from. Of course, my dilemmas reflect those of the Team, including, of course, their ambivalence about my working with them. This ambivalence was not just between members of the Team (the doctor and the nurse manager), but within the members as well (e.g. the doctor).

Ambivalence was also a feature of the nursing management in the District General Hospital. They were pleased and grateful that the courses were being run, and yet there were delays and nurses were given only the shortest time possible away from the wards.

This ambivalence, in turn, reflects the belief systems of the two systems. On the one hand, there is a strong conviction that certain practices are a necessary part of good health care, that clinical work should be supervised, that teams need to look at themselves, and that nurses should be aware of the emotional needs of the bereaved.

On the other hand, there is the belief that such practices are difficult to handle and should be avoided as they can lead to the emergence of conflict and painful feelings. The dilemma can be ignored by utilizing the manic defence and being too busy, which further avoids the recognition of conflict and painful feelings. I would not believe this to be unique to the systems described here!

CONCLUSIONS

There is no doubt too that nursing as an institution has and indeed is changing so as to recognize the importance of psychological factors in the patients with whom it works. This appears to carry over to nurses being more aware of the importance of their own psychological functioning and more prepared to look at it. Certainly there seems to be a recognition of the need nurses have for support and taking care of themselves.

This project was carried out at a time of tremendous organizational change in the NHS, in particular the setting up of self-governing NHS Trusts. It raises the question of who will be responsible for the type of work outlined in this chapter. At the outset of the project, it was apparent that there was a very real need for attending to the welfare of the bereaved and yet nothing had been done. As NHS reforms extend, the question as to who is responsible for what in the NHS may become even more problematic — the more so with the type of work described here, as there is no obvious immediate financial reward for responding to the needs of the bereaved. In addition, this project involved the cooperation of two NHS organizations, with their own managements. If the Community Unit had, at the time, been a Trust, would this cooperation have been possible? In addition, as Trusts become more autonomous and separate, will there be the same knowledge of what resources are available locally outside a particular Trust?

There is also the question of what place will be given to work related to the feelings of patients and staff. Will the Trusts have the opportunity to have a space where feelings can be acknowledged and reflected upon? If so, who will be given the role of managing the space? What this project illustrates is that the process of joint working and providing a space for thinking are not mutually exclusive.

CHAPTER NINE

Consultancy work in a closing psychiatric hospital

Alison Conning
Chartered Clinical Psychologist working in East Surrey

[This fascinating case study gives an account of internal consultancy offered within the context of the planned closure of a large psychiatric institution and associated resettling of its residents into the community.

The problems encountered by the consultant relate to the search for "the client" as the process of commissioning the consultant's task unexpectedly and frequently moves from one group of stakeholders to another. The resulting hierarchical shifts in the relationship between consultant and consultee are carefully tracked by Alison Conning against this maze of organizational change and of alliances falling apart, giving way to largely financially based partnerships of power.

The moral of this story appears to centre around the ability of the consultant to remain aware of the needs of the "end client", in this case the residents to be resettled, and to negotiate a strategic position that continues to keep these needs uppermost in the minds of the stakeholders. — Eds.]

Background

The context of the work described in this chapter is the closure of a large psychiatric asylum, which had, since the beginning of the century, been the focus of psychiatric care for a District Health Authority. In line with the international de-institutionalization movement (Bachrach, 1978), and British legislation shifting the focus of psychiatric care to "care in the community" (DoH, 1990), the District Health Authority had committed itself to developing a "community-based mental health service" and closing its psychiatric asylum. At the point at which this work was taken up, many parts of the hospital had already been closed and replaced off-site, and the time was ripe to set a final closure date.

A second important element to the context was the reorganization of the Mental Health Unit's management structure. The work was commissioned by the hub of the old management structure, just before it gave way to the new.

My role within the organization was to provide a psychology service to the District Rehabilitation and Long-Term Care service of the Mental Health Unit. During the reorganization of the Unit, psychology and the para-medical professions had lost their place in the management structure with the creation of a new breed of service managers who were not clinicians. At the time that the work described here was carried out, the new relationship between managers and clinicians was still being established.

SCOUTING

In November 1991 I was invited to join a working party that had been commissioned by the management team of the Mental Health Unit and charged with the following tasks:

1. to identify unmet housing needs for in-patients;
2. to identify future trends in housing needs due to population or service changes;
3. to propose a system to coordinate referrals to housing;
4. to present a series of papers that identify options to meet needs;
5. to stimulate developments from the independent sector, as well as to maintain the use of statutory provision.

The initial constitution of the group was: one representative from each of two voluntary sector Housing Associations (chairperson and secretary), an NHS manager, a member of the NHS Purchasing Authority, a representative of the Social Services, a representative of the Relatives Group, and a consultant psychiatrist. The constitution of the group shows that the management team recognized the need for several voluntary and statutory agencies to be involved with providing and supporting the future accommodation of the hospital in-patients, and this task was seen as a way of getting these agencies together as a catalyst for future development. For this reason, the task was not considered to be appropriate for an external consultant.

At the point at which I was invited to join the working party, they had met twice, discussed the tasks with which they had been commissioned, and come to the conclusion that they did not know how to proceed because they were not directly involved with the care of the patients. This was not made explicit to me at the time. The invitation to me was to join the working party, along with a senior registrar, as a replacement for the consultant psychiatrist, who had realized he was unable to be a member of the working party.

The implication could be that one senior registrar plus one psychologist equals a consultant psychiatrist, but I suspect that the joint invitation was to placate the medical hierarchy whilst recognizing the potential usefulness of a psychologist's skills. My agreement was given because the working party was going to make decisions about "my" patients, so it was better to be involved in the decisions than accept a *fait accompli*. I could have refused to join the working party but, although I was naive as to the exact nature of my task at this stage, it seemed likely that psychological skills, particularly of research, could be employed appropriately with the working party's remit. If the task had not been taken up by myself, I would have considered it vital that it should be taken up by somebody from my multi-disciplinary team, representing the clinicians working closest with this group of patients.

ENTRY
Enter the clinicians

Entry was at the point of the third meeting of the working party, after the consultant psychiatrist realized he could not attend and suggested an alternative. At this meeting, at which the tasks of the working party were discussed yet again, it became obvious that nobody knew how to proceed. Implicit in the discussion was the hope that the clinicians (the senior registrar and myself) would provide some guidance. It became clear that our role was to help the working party to identify how to proceed and to ensure that it did so. The task of the working party would have been much more difficult if we had not taken on this role, as the task required ease of access to information about patients. Although managers are usually assumed to have authority over clinicians, this illustrates the fragility of that hierarchy. Clinicians have knowledge, skills, and relationships that managers have access to only through them, giving clinicians a position of superiority in many situations. This raises the question of who my client was: the working party, or the Mental Health Unit management team? At this stage the client appeared to be the working party, as my task was to help them to complete the tasks for their client—the management team. In my own mind I was carrying out this piece of work as a servant of the *patients*, whose interests must always be uppermost.

CONTRACTING
Making the implicit explicit

As is often the case when one assumes a consultancy role after being given an implicit rather than an explicit invitation to do so, it was necessary to negotiate our "contract" in such a way as to allow the rest of the working group to save face. In Community Care all disciplines and agencies must work together, so the working party must present itself as a unit, completing the task together rather than continuing to be dominated by the NHS. It was appropriate for the NHS members to collude with this, as the other members would be able to give something in return at a later stage, such as houses from the Housing Associations.

The initial task was helping the working party to reach the decision that the first step was to carry out a survey of the future housing needs of all the remaining in-patients and then, when the rest of the working party had agreed that they did not know how to do this, volunteering to find an appropriate tool for information gathering. At this stage the contract was to find or design a tool for gathering the required information, and to bring it for the working party's amendment and approval.

DATA GATHERING 1
Re-inventing the wheel

It is rarely wise to spend time and energy inventing something when someone else has already done the work and is willing to share it with you. With this in mind, I went to consult a clinical psychologist from another hospital who had completed a similar task, and who had developed a suitable tool for the task.

The tool was appropriate but had the drawback of taking an average of 50 minutes per person to complete. As this would mean over 200 hours spent collecting data, without the "luxury" of someone whose time had been set aside for this task, this was not going to be practical. Fortunately, all was not lost.

Use of the device had resulted in the housing requirements of the people surveyed being fitted into six categories. It was decided that we would ask our staff to place each resident into one of these housing categories, which would provide sufficient information for a profile of the in-patients' housing requirements upon which to base planning.

CONTRACTING 2
Agreeing the next stage

The proposed form for data collecting was presented. Having been relieved to hand over the main task to the clinicians at the last meeting, the rest of the working party was now reluctant to relinquish a hold on the task. The negotiation here seemed to be about making the task something that everyone on the working party owned so that we were serving a common client — the management team. If the rest of the working party could not claim to have contributed to the group's task, then they could not share any praise given by the management team on its completion. Perhaps this struggle of ownership reflects the uncertainty about the ownership of patients/clients after the move to Care in the Community. Patients are no longer "owned" by the NHS as in-patients : Social Services should be taking the lead, with services provided by the voluntary sector and families as well as the NHS. The constitution of the group reflected these different agencies. Perhaps the members of the working party could not allow the NHS to be seen to be taking the lead in this piece of work as it would suggest that they were unable to fulfil the new responsibilities given to them by the National Health Service and Community Care Act (DoH, 1990). As psychologists working in rehabilitation are used to working in multi-disciplinary teams where recognition of the particular role played by an individual in achieving an end is not always given, it did not seem inappropriate or "foreign" to me to allow this multi-agency team to assume ownership of my work. To the extent that we were serving the same purpose, potential loss of recognition seemed unimportant. Nevertheless, other members of the working party had not completed their own task — that of bringing information about accommodation that was already planned by the voluntary sector and the management team.

After a heated and convoluted discussion about how the group should proceed, it was agreed that there should be a pilot study to evaluate the information-gathering form, and that members of the working party should send comments about the form before the next meeting.

DATA GATHERING 2
Pilot and amendments

The form was completed for twenty-nine residents of two wards, during one week, and the conclusions were that the staff were able to use the form without difficulty for all residents, and that it was not too time-consuming. The data were consistent with the decisions made about individuals in recent case conferences. Some of the housing categories were not relevant to this group of residents, but it was decided that those categories should not be removed because the patients in the pilot study were not necessarily typical of the entire in-patient population.

CONTRACTING 3
Enter the purchaser

The results of the pilot study were presented to the working party. Although the form had been used without problem, the working party suggested further minor amendments, again establishing it as their own. The representative of the Purchasing Authority was present at the meeting for the first time and presented a new dimension to the original task — that information should be provided about the source of funding for each patient, including private funds. Who is the client of the working party now? Is the Purchasing Authority the client of the management team? If the task shifted its primary focus to providing financial information, the work could then be owned by the Purchasing Authority and the rest of the working party might want to disown it.

Once more the working party felt overwhelmed and unsure about how to proceed. After a heated and angry discussion it was agreed that the survey should be carried out as planned, and that once completed the working party should meet again to discuss how to proceed. They did not want to hand over ownership to the Purchasing Authority. In their uncertainty about the new element to the task, they were happy to hand the data collection over to us, the clinicians, completely: our contract was once more with the working party.

The entry of the representative of the Purchasing Authority, and the anger and concern that her entry brought with it, illustrate the new dilemma with the NHS. As never before, money has become the guiding factor behind all services, with an ever-present conflict between the clinicians' desire to provide the best service for their clients and the purchaser's desire to keep within budget. Although purchasers and clinicians have a symbiotic relationship, ultimately the purchasers have the upper hand.

DATA GATHERING 3

A survey was carried out by the senior registrars and myself of the housing requirements of all the in-patients left in the hospital. Medical Records supplied a complete list of in-patients, with dates of birth, to guide the task. They were unable to provide what the Purchasing Authority wanted — the District of Origin.

DIAGNOSIS

The working party met to write a report on the results of the survey. Only three members of the original working party came — the chairperson, the secretary, and myself. The other clinician had left employment with this District Health Authority. The completion of the task was therefore being done by the people who would be providing most of the housing, and by myself, the person who had carried out the survey. The survey showed that there were 210 in-patients left, whose accommodation needs ranged from independent living to 24-hour care, with the majority requiring 24-hour care of some kind. When these individuals were matched to the accommodation that was already planned or coming on stream, 191 further places were required. The report was sent to the general manager, to report to the management team and decide the next move.

My contract with the working party had been fulfilled. The first stage of the working party's contract with the management team had been fulfilled, but had the management team fulfilled their contract with the Purchasing Authority?

The general manager's response to the report was to call a meeting with the authors of the report and a representative of an agency who had been commissioned by the Regional Health Authority to help each District develop their mental health strategy. The focus of the meeting was to match the results of our survey to the plans for reprovision which had been drawn up by the new management structure. The hidden agenda, as I discovered later, was that in the switch over from the old to the new management structure, the piece of work commissioned from the working party had been forgotten, and the arrival of its report had been an embarrassment, as plans had gone ahead without the benefit of the information it produced.

The outcome of the meeting was that I was asked by the general manager to meet with a member of the Development Agency, to bring the survey (now four months old) up to date, to match its findings to the plans, and to add some information required by the Purchasing Authority. There was no doubt in my mind that our survey was a more appropriate source of information about clients' needs than the reprovision plans, so I aimed to mould the plans to our data and not vice versa.

Just before the task was completed, the representative of the Development Agency left the county, stating that he would pass the task on to a colleague who would contact me. A few weeks later, I was contacted by the Purchasing Authority with a request for a specific piece of information: the cost of the future housing requirements of the in-patients belonging to this District, which is what they thought to be the outcome of my task. Suddenly, and without my knowledge, a new contract had been negotiated for me by someone else, and I had a new client, the Purchasing Authority. Once more the purchasers were reasserting their authority by re-introducing financial considerations. However, they were unable to work out the cost of future housing without access to my data, once more illustrating the symbiosis of the relationship but with the purchasers having the upper hand. If providing this information would help to ensure future housing for our patients, I was willing to give it.

The task was completed, to the satisfaction of the Purchasing Authority, with the help of a second member of the Development Agency. In return for the data I gave her, I was able to influence, through discussion, the document she was writing on the future of our health services.

EVALUATION

This work has shown that during the process of consulting, the contract can change one or more times. This begs the question, "why"? Here are some speculative answers.

1. In the changing NHS, the roles of, and relationships between purchasers and providers, between provider managers and provider clinicians, are still being negotiated. Where a piece of work is relevant to staff from all parties, each will want to influence the nature of the work, but the exact mechanism for doing this has not yet been established. The result is that different parties attempt to influence the work at different, and perhaps inappropriate, moments. The party that has influenced the work most recently becomes the client.

2. Psychologists often become internal consultants not by prior invitation, but by offering their own skills when others are floundering. This means that the contract is often implicit rather than explicit, and so it is vulnerable to change without negotiation. In the new business climate of the NHS, psychologists will need to be proactive in increasing other people's knowledge of their skills, and ensuring that contracts are made explicit.

3. Only once a task is undertaken by a consultant are its possibilities for usefulness completely uncovered, particularly when the skills of the consultant have not been known to potential clients and the work has not been formally contracted. Once the possibilities are clear, new clients may want to state their claim on the work.

Despite the changing contract, the internal consultancy carried out by myself in this piece of work was via the "expert role". This seemed to come about because other members of the working party had neither the skills, nor the time, nor the ease of access to mental health staff needed to collect the information required for the working party's tasks. At the point of my entry, they appeared to be looking for an "expert" who would know what to do. This suggests that sufficient thought was not given to the initial constitution of the group by the management team.

CONCLUSIONS

1.   It is difficult to say whether the contract had been completed successfully, because from my point of view what the contract was, and with whom, changed at each stage of the process. The working party did not complete all of its original tasks, but as the management team that had commissioned its services no longer existed, this was now irrelevant.

I completed each of the contracts that emerged at different stages of the process, but the task would have been quicker and easier if I had been directly commissioned by the management team or by the Purchasing Authority. The working party slowed the process down, but this may have been a necessary cost for the gain of the involvement of the housing associations, which are needed to provide and manage some of the future housing provision.

The chairperson and the secretary of the working party were both pleased with the work, which in their eyes was completed as a team, and they have each, separately, asked me to carry out another piece of work with them. Both members of the Development Agency came to regard me as an ally and gave me access to useful information. Although they were working for the purchaser, the time I spent with them allowed me to influence their views on the future of our health District and so influence the document they were writing for the purchasers. I may have gained status in the eyes of the management team by the work with the Development Agency but it is difficult to parcel out all the elements that may have contributed to my rising profile.

2.   The process illustrates the fact that in an organization as complicated as the NHS, who one's client is may not always be clear. When an organization is layered, a contract with someone several layers down means that implicitly one has a contract with the people in the layers above. The problems that can arise from this may in part be solved by an open and formal contract being negotiated between the commissioning agent and the psychologist (Brunning &

Huffington, 1990), but this contract may need to be renegotiated, even with a different commissioning agent, if the requirements of one of the "layers" change. At the moment the "layers" in the NHS, at least in this District, do not always connect: relevant information is not always passed from one layer to another; and the roles appropriate to each layer, and how a layer should relate to another which is some distance away, are not always clear. This may be to do with the newness of the present structure in the NHS: relationships are still being negotiated, and old relationships are difficult to give up. One result of this "newness" may be that managers are sometimes reluctant to reveal their actions to clinicians, in the belief that secret knowledge imparts authority and power.

3. The results of the survey provided data to feed into the management structure's planning process. It was not within my remit to develop their plans—I can only respond to the plans that they make.

4. Despite the fact that I was brought into the task as someone close to the clients, the latter were not involved in the work. This was a deliberate strategy aimed at separating the role of the working party from the role of clinical teams. Throughout my involvement, I tried to make it clear that it was only appropriate for the working party to provide a profile of likely housing requirements. Matching individual clients to actual facilities was properly the role of the clinical teams working with the clients.

5. When a large organization is going through the process of changing its structure, the confusion and uncertainty created by the transition can affect the work of individuals in all parts of the organization. However, psychologists do not have to be passive recipients of the confusion and uncertainty: transition points can be used by the psychologist to establish his or her place and usefulness within the organization.

6. The difficulties arising from an implicit consultancy contract may be overcome by an open and formal contract being negotiated between the commissioning agent and the psychologist. On the

other hand, in a changing organization, the limitations of a formal consultancy contract may mean that the psychologist is unable to respond to new tasks or challenges as they are created. Clarity may sometimes limit creativity!

7.   The National Health Service and Community Care Act (DoH, 1990) requires that statutory, voluntary, and private sector agencies work together to provide a service to the long-term mentally ill. The work described here illustrates an attempt at cooperation between these agencies, and responsibilities are still being negotiated. As these relationships evolve, it is likely that the skills of psychologists will be seen to be useful to all the agencies, resulting in many opportunities for psychologists to take up consultancy roles.

WITHDRAWAL

The work ended with the completion of the work for the Purchasing Authority. The other tasks originally given to the working party were no longer required by the new management structure. The last stage of my task provided information about the thing most important to the new NHS — the cost of providing care.

PART FOUR

INTERNAL CONSULTANCY IN EDUCATION

Introduction

Maureen Fox
Consultant Child Psychologist

Over the past 25 years a plethora of legislation has flooded schools and institutions of higher education. Whilst some of this legislation has been viewed by educators as at best "misguided", other aspects of it have been supported and welcomed by teachers. Many staff have appreciated the increasing involvement of parents, applauded the autonomy of locally managed schools, and valued the introduction of a national curriculum.

What has been remarkable is how badly the government has managed these changes. Lack of consultation, contradictory communications, peremptory shifts in policy, unrealistic deadlines, and the absence of evaluation have all contributed to the creation of an atmosphere of confusion and mistrust. One of the repercussions of this approach has been that the implementation of these reforms, including those aspects which would otherwise have been carried out with enthusiasm by teachers, has been rendered unnecessarily complicated and difficult.

Whilst it has been appropriate to resist and to continue to resist the more unenlightened aspects of these reforms, nevertheless many schools have found themselves empowered in a way that until very recently they never felt possible. These are schools who have responded to the changes by readily assuming control and taking their own authority.

One of the major consequences of this acquisition of power has been a shift in the role and structure of management in schools and in the duties and responsibilities of individual teachers. The assumption of these new tasks and functions has required schools to redesign their internal structures and lines of communication in keeping with the requirements of the new arrangements. Staff are now required to contribute to policy making and planning from a position of authority which is unfamiliar and which many experience as simultaneously challenging and daunting.

Governors, senior management, and teachers are involved in the management of change and in its monitoring and evaluation. There has been a significant shift in the balance of power between headteachers and governing bodies. Many schools now see consultation and accountability within and between sub-systems as a prerequisite. The introduction of appraisal and review provides a forum within which all staff have the opportunity for involvement and influence.

Schools exist to serve the young people in their community and provide them with the best possible opportunities for education. It is only through the competent management of resources, both human and material, that these aims and objectives can be achieved and our responsibility to future generations adequately discharged.

CHAPTER TEN

Consulting to a new headteacher on developing the role

Bryony Howe
Senior Educational Psychologist
in an East London borough

[This clear and concise case study addresses the difficulties of succession for a deputy headteacher assuming a headship in the same school. Approached within the context of her own learning on a consultancy course, Bryony Howe was also moving from the role of educational psychologist to consultant. This changed the nature of the hierarchical relationship between headteacher and consultant and enabled Bryony Howe to negotiate a process of exploration with the headteacher, which proved to be mutually beneficial. She was able to suspend her role of educational psychologist to the school while this process took place, but she found that the consultancy changed relationships in such a way that not only did the head adjust better to her new role, but that the consultant's educational psychology role was also informed in a new way. In this respect, consultant and consultee both made an effective transition to new roles! — Eds.]

SCOUTING

I have worked for my current Local Education Authority (LEA) as a part-time educational psychologist (EP) since its conception in April 1989. My role involves offering a regular psychological service to a small group of (LEA) schools and a service to parents and children living in a defined area of this inner-city borough. All schools are allocated a certain amount of time and visited on a regular basis. Most of my schools are mainstream, but I have one special school for children with severe learning difficulties, which I visit once a fortnight.

Since the introduction of the 1981 Education Act, more and more of the work has become statutory, involving reviews of children's progress and their placement at the school. This has led to a feeling of frustration both for the school and for myself about the lack of time for other ways of working. During September 1992, I attended a three-day consultancy course organized by the Tavistock Clinic. One of the requirements was that we should put some of the principles into practice and conduct our own project. The consultancy therefore needed to be set up quickly. As a result I felt I would have to use a school that I was already visiting on a fairly regular basis. The special school was the only school that fitted that requirement—but the headteacher had not approached me with a problem.

NEGOTIATING ENTRY/ESTABLISHING THE CONTRACT

There were two dilemmas for me in setting up a consultancy in this way. First, the request for consultancy did not come from the headteacher. Rather, I told her about the consultation course I had attended and asked her whether she might consider working in this way, on an area that was presenting problems. The headteacher's motivation and willingness to work in a different way might therefore have been a problem.

Second, since I had been visiting the school for the previous five years, expectations had been built up about the ways in which I worked — usually focusing on the needs of individual children or the concerns of their teachers. It might have been difficult for the headteacher and the school to modify their expectations and adapt to a change in role.

In particular, as the consultancy sessions were held in school, I might have found it difficult to keep them clear both of requests for my more usual ways of working and of interruptions.

However, as the EP for the school, there was a common knowledge between us about the LEA. I knew something about the school, I knew quite a number of the parents and children, and I had already established working relationships with many of the teachers. Thus, I felt I was already working from a basis of trust. As it was, the headteacher seemed to welcome the change and appreciated being asked to keep a space free of interruptions. She herself was a new headteacher.

The client

The client, Sarah, was appointed to the headship about six months prior to the start of the project. Before that, she had worked as the deputy headteacher in the school. She had always maintained that she did not want the headship, but she was a popular appointment with the governors and staff. Although my previous contacts with her had always been good, my working relationship during the previous five years had been largely confined to the original headteacher, who had been at the school since its conception. My relationship with Sarah, particularly in her role as headteacher, was therefore a relatively new one. My expectations of Sarah were very positive — that we would be able to work well together and that I might be able to offer support. Although she probably expected me to continue to work in the way I had always done, the fact that we had not worked closely together before made it easier to adapt to a change in my role. I think, in this instance by chance, it also suited her needs at this stage.

What is the consultant coming in to do?

We established that there was a particular issue with which Sarah would welcome some help.

This was done through an initial telephone call and further discussion, followed by a letter detailing what I was offering to do.

This established:

1. that I would help her look at issues involved in the problem she was presenting.
2. the three appointment times, at regular fortnightly intervals.
3. that during the first three sessions I would help to analyse the difficulties with her and see in what way I might be able to help.

What is the responsibility of the client?

Sarah agreed to let the senior management team know what we were doing and also to keep free the times that we had negotiated.

ANALYSIS OF THE PROBLEM

The presenting problem was to do with the Annual Review forms. These are a formal way of reporting back to both parents and the LEA on the progress of children with Statements of Special Educational Need (SEN). Although the LEA already has Annual Review forms, the school had developed its own versions, under the direction of the previous headteacher, which it felt were more helpful. These had in the past been held up as a model of good practice by the adviser for Special Educational Needs. Sarah's concern was that although the staff felt the forms were useful to them, they did not now meet the LEA requirements — namely, to involve children and parents in their completion and to record their views, and to refer to levels of the National Curriculum.

However, during the first session it became clear that this concern might represent underlying issues that were making it difficult for Sarah to move forward. This became clearer when we looked at options for change. Sarah had only considered adding on to the current form. She had deliberately avoided thinking about devising a new one, since changing the form, she anticipated, would lead to trouble with her staff. "Who would do it, and with whose support? In this school things are done as a team."

She agreed that we should spend the next two sessions looking at the organization of the school and the support structures within it, and that we should review Sarah's position within the larger organization and where her support was coming from.

My hypothesis at this stage was that changing the Annual Review forms represented Sarah's ambivalence about making the transition from deputy headteacher to headteacher. If she changed the Annual Review forms, then, since they had been created by the previous headteacher, she would be taking on the role of headteacher. However, her belief that "change leads to trouble" meant that any change would lead to trouble with her staff, and she was used to a role of support, of keeping "all the staff happy". As a headteacher, difficult and sometimes unwelcome decisions had to be made.

If the forms were not changed, then she would fall foul of legal and LEA requirements—and as a newly appointed headteacher she wanted to get things right. She might be able to change the forms given support, but no replacement deputy headteacher had yet been appointed, so where was her support to come from?

I think this was why this consultation was well-timed. Sarah could not turn to her teachers in this instance, and there was a gap in support, both internally and externally.

DATA GATHERING AND DIAGNOSIS

Data gathering included the following sources (not in any order of priority):

* *My knowledge of the school and borough, and use of information gathered from my regular visits to the school*

- *Meetings with the headteacher*
- *Organizational map*

The drawing of an organizational map proved extremely helpful in establishing the existing support structures and organization both inside and outside the school. In fact, I think I learnt more about the organization of the school and relationships in it within three sessions than I had learnt in the previous five years.

Although always acknowledging the importance of context for the child and family, I had never previously focused on the relevance of the structure of the organization to the individual in it. The drawing of the map heightened my awareness of the importance of clarifying roles within the school and locating sources of support.

In drawing it, I asked Sarah to think about:

1. who was in the organization (both at school and in the LEA), and what that person's place was in that organization;
2. who was accountable to whom;
3. issues of race and gender;
4. sources of support.

Gaps were immediately apparent to both of us and questions arose naturally, not just for me but also for Sarah. She became aware not only of the gaps in support, but that, in the absence of a deputy headteacher and an inspector, most of her support was coming from her personal assistant. As a result, she set aside regular times to spend with her personal assistant in the same way as we had done.

At the same time, Sarah recognized that there were limits to what her personal assistant could offer and that the latter's support could not replace that of a deputy and inspector. It became clear that lack of support from the LEA was affecting her management of the school. From being unwilling to ask for support (because of a belief that she should be able to cope without), she moved to a point where she expressed her anger directly to the assistant director and chief inspector and insisted that the deputy-headteacher post be advertised externally as soon as possible.

The lack of clarity of roles within the school also became apparent. It seemed that particularly amongst the incentive "C" post-holders — the senior management — the teachers' job descriptions no longer matched the jobs they were doing nor the responsibilities they held, nor was it clear which teachers had a responsibility for support and to whom.

This led Sarah to consider her difficulties in adjusting to her new role as headteacher.

As deputy headteacher, Sarah had unofficially taken on the role of supporting everybody. Staff continued to expect this, yet Sarah was finding it increasingly difficult to meet these needs — both because she found it emotionally exhausting, added to the new demands of being headteacher, and because this led to conflicts with her management role.

Awareness of these difficulties resulted in her clarifying roles. Job descriptions were rewritten in consultation with senior management.

* * *

- *Meetings with the headteacher*
- *Headteacher's experience of the meetings*

As a result of her experience, Sarah began to question her belief that she should be able to cope without support.

I asked her:

"How can you support your staff if you are not getting support for yourself?"

"What are your feelings about not getting support?"

"Do you have a right to support?"

"How did your colleagues react when you asked for support from the hierarchy?"

She began to insist upon the support from the LEA that had previously not been forthcoming. This has begun to have some effect. She acknowledged her need for space for her own development and attended a course in Cambridge without worrying too much about how the school would cope in her absence. She also began to recognize her staff's need for support and need to become aware that there were sources of support other than herself.

She redistributed support roles amongst her senior teachers so that she was no longer supporting all the staff.

* * *

• *My experience of the meetings*

The organizational map had exposed a long-standing difficulty with a particular member of staff, Hilary, of which I had not been aware. The problem appeared to be exacerbated by Sarah's knowledge of a "secret" in Hilary's past.

My hypothesis was that this represented the dilemma between managing people and conducting personal relationships with them: that personal relationships affect management. In this case, Sarah's belief that she should support Hilary was affecting herself, as the rest of the staff found her handling of Hilary difficult to understand.

It also exposed the lack of support from the LEA, since there was no one to turn to to ask about procedures.

Analysis and feedback of my own feelings, after Sarah had explained the difficulties with Hilary, was helpful both to me and to Sarah. I fed back to Sarah how I had felt after the session — in a tangle, unable to think straight. Also, how unwilling I had been to think about the session again until I had to. I had found myself becoming quite overwhelmed and muddled by what Sarah told me.

Since she identified with these feelings, this feedback brought Sarah considerable relief. She used a similar metaphor to describe how she was "beginning to untangle things a little at a time".

She agreed that knowing Hilary's secret was preventing her from dealing with Hilary in the way she wanted and was also affecting her relationships with the rest of the staff. Whilst she wanted to avoid conflict with Hilary, the result was conflict with others.

Having recognized how muddled the situation with Hilary made people feel, I was better able to remain objective and to consider, during a meeting with Hilary, how it was that she achieved this effect. It became clear that there were a number of things that she did that tended to overwhelm and undermine those who listened to her. One thing was to dash at high speed from one problem, issue, or observation to another, so that nothing was ever resolved. Another was to refer to her greater experience and knowledge, in this case on autism. A third was to go off sick.

Feedback from my meeting with Hilary to Sarah helped both of us think about new ways of managing Hilary.

By our next meeting, Sarah had decided that she would give someone else line-management responsibility for supporting Hilary, that if Sarah made herself available to Hilary, she would set limits to the time she could have and keep a written record of what went on; and that she would encourage her to develop her own sources of support. In this case Hilary set up meetings with the staff she was working with. Finally, Sarah organized a course on autism for all her staff since this was an area of need identified by many other teachers in the school.

It became very clear that without resolving this difficulty, which was based on her belief that she could make everybody happy, we could not have moved forward. The problem was quite over-whelming to Sarah, preventing her from thinking about anything else.

From my point of view, being let into the school's "secret" seemed an acknowledgement of the trust that had built up between us.

* * *

- *Detailed notes kept of the interviews, which helped to expose the possible belief system*
- *Meetings with a consultation partner, and a consultant from outside the system altogether, which helped me to refocus on the process and belief system and avoid becoming bogged down in detail and practicality*

INTERVENTION

The consultancy process appeared to result in Sarah resolving many of the underlying difficulties in her own way and by herself. By the end of the third session, although difficulties remained, we agreed we could return to the presenting problem of the Annual Review forms.

However this no longer seemed to present major difficulties. Sarah was still concerned that there would be trouble with her teachers but she was now prepared to direct them. "I can't make all the staff happy — I've learnt that."

We used a fourth session to focus on the Annual Review forms, to consider how Sarah was going to present the changes to her staff, and to consider possible difficulties that might arise.

In the event, there were very few problems. One major change — namely, the timing of the reviews — which Sarah had been particularly worried about introducing, was positively welcomed. These were now to be staggered over the year, instead of being completed as a block during the summer term.

EVALUATION

Although many of her problems remained, Sarah felt our meetings had allowed her to gain understanding of her difficulties. She felt our discussions had "opened things up". She had "enough ideas to take her forward". She was able to tackle some of the difficulties, "to untangle little bits at a time", by changing some of her beliefs — for example, that requests for support would be regarded as weakness and that change would always be seen negatively. She is now beginning to feel that her needs have some legitimacy; she is beginning to feel that she has a right to support, not as a luxury, but to help her carry out her responsibilities more effectively; and she is beginning to ask for this support from those who should be supporting her. There appears to be an increasing acknowledgement that all staff need support, and that, as well as giving responsibility to senior management, all staff can support one another. Sarah is currently considering the gap in support for ancillary staff.

Sarah has begun to clarify for herself her new role as headteacher, and to develop strategies for making this clearer to those around her. The appointment of a new deputy headteacher is a tremendous relief, but she is also much clearer about what his new responsibilities will be.

All these changes have been positively reinforced by comments from an external consultant, temporarily appointed by the LEA, who told Sarah this term that he was impressed by the clarity of the school's organizational structure.

I have noticed an increase in teachers' requests via Sarah to discuss their concerns about individual children with me (although this may be because there has been some time to do this). However, I am much more alert to possible underlying difficulties and tend now to consider the organization and their part in it, something I would probably not have done before.

Sarah has said she feels it would be helpful to continue working in this way this term and has also said that other teachers might find it useful to work in this way. The difficulty will be keeping a regular space clear, as well as keeping the focus on just one issue. We discussed meeting outside school as one way around these difficulties, but Sarah preferred to keep the meetings inside school.

I feel that the experience of the consultancy has brought about a fundamental change in my thinking, both about my role as an educational psychologist and in my approach to referrals.

Whilst I always recognized the importance of the school context, I had no clear strategies to help me find out more about it and, having found out more, I was unsure about how I could best help an organization to change.

Focusing on the beliefs and culture of the organization, together with the relationships within it, has given me a framework within which to work, leading to a different set of questions eliciting a different set of answers. These questions have helped me to avoid being overwhelmed by detail and have helped me to understand things in a different way.

I feel more confident about slowing things down and not coming up with solutions straightaway—always a danger as an educational psychologist. I believe I am now much clearer about why some problems cannot be resolved by meeting the client's initial request and how indeed these problems may be exacerbated unless one spends time reflecting on underlying issues. Requests for in-service training seem often to be a case in point.

I now feel much more confident about the usefulness of listening and questioning, and particularly about asking difficult or confrontational questions. They have become much more purposeful, much less personal. I have found I have used my experience of consultancy to reflect on my own organization, in which I work as a senior educational psychologist. There are currently a number of outstanding unfilled senior posts within the organization, and I have become increasingly aware of the pressures this has placed on members of the team. My experience of consultancy has made me look at the issue of support in my own organization. Coincidentally (or not?), this has now become a heated issue in the team. Further questioning has revealed that it is almost certainly an issue within the management structure of the LEA.

Within the team, some changes have begun to be made. Although there is much further to go, the fact is that the issue is now in the open.

The dilemmas of working as an internal consultant remain.

In the face of growing demands for Statutory Assessments of the needs of individual children, it is difficult to set aside the time to look at organizational issues on a regular basis, and to persuade headteachers that there is much to be gained. Once the benefits have been experienced, however, a headteacher may feel it is worthwhile. As far as Sarah is concerned, both of us want to make time to continue to work in this way.

As far as educational psychologists are concerned, consultancy may save a great deal of wasted time and effort. However, even if one is unable to offer formal consultancy, the experience of working in a consultative way affects the way one thinks about and approaches problems, which is impossible to confine to set times.

RE-EVALUATION

The new deputy headteacher has now taken up his post, releasing Sarah from some of the practical pressures of day-to-day responsibilities. His expertise on the National Curriculum has been an added bonus.

Although we have not set up a further, formal contract, I feel this has been more to do with us having reached a period of consolidation, rather than the result of the arrival of a new deputy headteacher. Since Easter, Sarah has been working on refining the Annual Review forms, drawing up a rota for their completion, and training staff in their use. This has been highly successful. The forms now meet the needs of both the school and the LEA. Parents, children, and professionals have been drawn in. The reviews are no longer just school reports. My role in all this has been to provide information about what the LEA wants.

The proposed appointment of a new adviser for Special Educational Needs may have a more significant effect on my use as a consultant. However, I will be alert to future opportunities. My feeling now is that Sarah knows what I can offer and that I must wait for a new issue to be raised by her.

CHAPTER ELEVEN

Exploring difference: consulting to a Jewish secondary school

Liz Kennedy
Educational Psychologist, Child and Family Department,
Tavistock Clinic, and City of Westminster Psychological Service

[This eloquent case study is concerned with a self-selected group of staff within a school, often the "working unit" of the consultancy process. Liz Kennedy clearly illustrates the double-bind for herself as consultant in setting up this group. In negotiating a contract for running a group that could only be set up within the individualized belief system of the school and without the participation of the management, she engaged in a high-risk strategy in terms of the success of the project in affecting the whole organization.

The group became preoccupied with issues of power, management, difference, and the rivalry that emerged between the consultant and the headteacher. Liz Kennedy was, however, able to use these themes to promote a sense of group responsibility, which did have an effect on the staff culture as a whole and on management, in that the headteacher became involved in the process by asking for consultancy around his role. The recursive relationships between the group, the whole school, and the wider context around the school are clearly illustrated. — Eds.]

BACKGROUND

I n this case study, I intend to describe my experience of working with a self-selected staff group in a provincial Jewish secondary school with a staff of 50. I hope to show how this small group's preoccupations and work concerns reflected organizational issues for the school as a whole. The work they did with me over a school year allowed the institution to be made aware of some powerful forces that affected the lives of all within it, and which were reflected in organizational structures and processes. Not all the issues we discussed necessarily led to structural or procedural changes, either as the group proceeded or after it had finished, but for those who participated it seemed to help to make sense of the emotional as well as the professional and social demands being made on them.

SCOUTING

Of particular interest to me was the way in which I addressed and learned about internal consultancy and the legitimacy issues it raises. As the educational psychologist (EP) attached to the school, I had had an ongoing relationship with them for several years. Apart from the inspectorate and the education welfare officer, I was the only other "outside" county professional going into the school on a regular basis.

Relations with the County Council seemed distant, and a widely held view was of an anonymous, unsupportive administration at County Hall. Much closer relations were evident with the religious community, to whom considerable outward deference was shown.

133

It had been particularly difficult for the school to accept that I could work at different levels within the institution, wanting, I felt, to see my client group as only the children and parents. Defining who is the client, and therefore what the primary task of an intervention is, is a common thorny issue for EPs. It can be problematic when one gets caught up either in competing "conceptual" demands between the levels within the institution or in actual overt conflicts occurring between the different working groups. The overlaps and confusions between pupils, parents, staff, senior management, governors, and the wider religious community was a particular area of concern for the school and had always meant that I had to be very clear about my "primary client" and "primary task" for each piece of work I undertook.

The school is sited within an industrial estate. The building had been the object of break-ins and arson attacks; the County Council had therefore recently enclosed the site behind a high wall. Parent volunteers were responsible for monitoring entry and exit, and identity and appointment had to be established before you could be admitted. All the staff at the school were Jewish, and the fact that I am very obviously not seemed to me to be important . At the time of the group initiative, I had been visiting the school for a number of years and had had some involvement with almost all staff.

ENTRY

The request for a group arose out of a series of in-service training (inset) sessions that I ran on behavioural management. It had been my suggestion that inset made a more economical use of my time than individual consultation about a series of children with difficult behaviour. The inset sessions were tightly structured in terms of both time and content, and staff were required to sign a contract undertaking to complete the assignments and to arrive on time. In discussions about the children, links had been made with staff behaviour, with such strong worries expressed that a request was made to explore this further. Having felt some responsibility for helping the training group explore links within the institution around the behaviour of various groups, I had an interest in seeing this work through and agreed to consider running a work discussion group for interested staff.

It seemed to me that the request for a group was closely connected with both the content and the structure of the inset series. A focus on managing behaviour, albeit children's, in a positive and consistent manner, appeared to highlight the contrast with some of the staff behaviour and made maintenance of the status quo impossible if any of the ideas from the course were to be put into practice. The course had introduced a novel way of viewing problem behaviours that was quite dissonant with the prevailing beliefs, which tended to attach difficulties and problems to individuals rather than seeing them in a wider context. With hindsight, it seems as if the work-discussion group offered staff a welcome relief from the loneliness of enforced autonomy and individual responsibility.

CONTRACTING

Although I felt that this was a legitimate request in terms of *content*, the legitimacy of the process and the structure needed clarification. Negotiating a contract proved deceptively simple. As part of the inset feedback to the headteacher, I reported on the general discussion and the request I had received. He was delighted to hear that I was prepared to offer a work-discussion group but made it clear that he did not want to take part himself. He was largely unwilling (or unable) to discuss the potential divisiveness of running a closed group for only certain members of staff; he was also unhappy to discuss any potential competition that might arise over authority issues between us in relation to the participants. My failure to clarify my concerns sufficiently around these issues was to prove a central preoccupation of the group members.

Given the group's only partly unconscious wish to "knock" management, in the person of the headteacher, it was perhaps not surprising that he did not wish to take part. My view of the system was of one in which issues were personalized, and that change was the prerogative of the individual rather than structures or procedures being created to promote or manage change. The hierarchical nature of the institution served to protect the headteacher from group pressure as competition was in-built and self-perpetuating. Given that this was my view, I reasoned that the group would not run with him in it, and I felt that the risk of splitting between him and me could be addressed in the group.

Following my discussion with the headteacher, there was a staff meeting in which the idea of the group was raised. As a result, I was formally requested to outline a contract for a weekly group. It was agreed by my own line management that I would offer weekly sessions for three terms, which would be separate and distinct from my contracted visits as school EP. This was to be justified by the hope that the group might help to address some of the whole issues around behavioural management (a high proportion of my referrals fell into this category). The group was to be voluntary, with a closed membership, and was to be held after school. The contract was clearly that the group was primarily aimed to benefit and support the individuals within it, but general observations and concerns would be fed back either via a verbal report to the headteacher or by a written report to him for general circulation. Therefore, the group was set up within the (individualized) belief system of the school.

The task of the group was to examine issues of concern as they arose for individuals, and for the group to help that individual explore and clarify the nature of his or her relationship to the institution (and the group) around the problem. The discussions were to be work- and task-centred, and personal revelations were to be discouraged. It was my own hope that we would gain a far greater understanding of the complex dynamics operating within the institution, so that we could all focus more effectively on our primary task.

DATA GATHERING/DIAGNOSIS/INTERVENTION

Issues and themes

The final membership of the group consisted of nine female teaching staff, even though the gender mix on the entire staff was roughly equal. In a Jewish school and with a female, non-Jewish consultant, this issue became one of great importance in the difficulties that the group had in dealing with *difference*. A particular aspect of this —"outsiders" — was one that the group continued to grapple with in relation to me; the issue of difference, or lack of differentiation, was possibly the central theme over the year.

The theme of "difference" emerged in several guises. Four particular topics kept re-emerging, with minor transformations, and I will illustrate two of these by describing two meetings in detail. The topics can be simplified for the purposes of this study as follows:

- Insiders and Outsiders;
- Splitting and Fragmenting as against Cohesion;
- Difference and Assimilation;
- Time and Space Boundaries.

My role in the group was largely one of facilitator, but one who made use of feelings and their connection to behaviour in and out of the group. The format we agreed on was that each week a member would bring a concern which the group as a whole would help her think about in relation to the three ongoing strands:

- the development of the individual;
- the development of the group;
- their relationship to the wider institution.

Working within a psychodynamic and systemic framework, it was my intention to explore meaning, both unconscious and conscious, but also to try constantly to locate concerns in the widest possible context. This was a very ambitious task, especially working within what was for the group a totally unusual setting. How I managed, or failed, to keep these levels constantly in mind increasingly emerged as an issue between myself and the (absent) headteacher, in which at times I felt I was set up in competition in terms of authority in an unhelpful and largely negative way.

Using the structure of individual presentation throughout, my role did change quite significantly, however, over the lifetime of the group. Initially, I was active in questioning without commenting and in discouraging judgemental remarks. A constant feature of my role was the need for vigilance about what was happening in the group and its connection to the content of the presentation. Group behaviour towards me tended to oscillate between dependence (for advice or answers), anger (at my comments or lack of them), and independent thinking—a capacity that developed later in the sessions and which, ironically, made me feel redundant (almost certainly a "good thing!").

Two group sessions

I want to give an account of two of the group sessions, one from early in the group's life and one from the middle of the second term.

Session 3: "Time"

I arrived and set out the room. The group were all late, and people were arriving up to ten minutes after the start. Nobody appeared to want to present a current concern, and a series of desultory remarks were made about events of the day (fire drill, visit from a Rabbi). Finally one of the group commented on how hard it felt to get started. I asked if it had been difficult for people to come today given all these events, commenting on the ragged beginning and lateness. After a short silence someone said, "Its just like this at assembly". Most of the group assented, and on asking what she meant I received the following account in which all the group members actively and animatedly contributed. Assembly started at 9.20, but it was "usual" for tutor groups to still be arriving at 9.45. The headteacher was often late himself, and no one could recall assembly ever starting on time. Those groups who had arrived at 9.20 were frequently restless and difficult to manage by the time things did start. Often the children and staff were publicly rebuked by the headteacher, the first for their behaviour, the others for their inability to manage it. Those staff to whom this had happened were very resentful of the headteacher but were equally furious with their colleagues. Within the group there were some quite angry exchanges, until one person reminded everybody that not all the school clocks were coordinated. The mood of the group changed quite markedly after this remark, with several people commenting on the impossibly mixed message of running a school around time boundaries when the clocks were not synchronized. They decided that at the next staff meeting they would point out how unnecessary conflicts were arising between head and staff, staff and staff, staff and children, and children and children. One of the two deputies present decided to take it on herself to ask the caretaker to alter the clocks. As it was nearly time for the group to finish, I asked them to think about their experience of me managing their time boundary strictly. Several vigorous denials of any similarity between the discussion and the process within the group followed. However no one was ever late again without giving prior warning!

It seemed to me that this session focused on difference, particularly in *status*. I had been "invited" to compete with the head, to set and enforce boundaries around the sessions, and to scold them for their "non-attendance". Had I taken them to task early in the session for their lateness, I am certain that they would have experienced it as very personal and persecuting: I feel sure that such a comment would have usurped any possibility of their owning the problem and setting about solving it as a group.

Session 17: "Exposure"

Apologies were given on behalf of one of the deputies who was "sorting out a crisis". Apparently two girls had been exposing themselves for money. This announcement was greeted with much laughter by the group, and I felt there was a hysterical feel at this point. After several minutes I asked whether sometimes they felt as if they were "exposing themselves" in the group. Nobody responded to this comment, but one of the year-7 staff started talking about the new parents visiting the school. Several members had been angered by the way the parents had drifted into their lessons unannounced, and, for some, this had been experienced as an intrusion.

The deputy arrived, full of her management of the two girls, and once again the group laughed about the incident. At this point the deputy spoke very angrily about the headteacher, who had "left her to it" to sort out the problem with the parents. Once again I hazarded a comment that some of the things in the group might leave individuals feeling vulnerable and exposed, and I wondered if they felt that I just left them to get on with it. This time my comment was heard and several members started to complain about the headteacher, whom they felt utterly failed to plan, consult, or follow through on actions. The visit by new parents was cited as a case in point. There had been no timetable, parents were allowed to wander about the school as they wished, and some were abandoned in mid-visit. The group were furious that the parents should see how disorganized things were, and several members felt affronted that the parents had observed lessons unscheduled. Some of the most vociferous complaints had been about one department (of which the head was a teaching member) who had organized displays and talks during the day at published times. One of the group commented on how disruptive her teaching group had found the visit and how she had felt some childish pleasure (triumph) when none of the children wanted to show the visitors their work. I was compared favourably to the head, my style was very different, always trying to understand and name what was going on.

I commented on how they sometimes experienced the group as a place where they could talk openly about such negative feelings, but I reminded them that I too was an outsider (in every way) and that they had to relate to me outside the group in a different way. I wondered whether outsiders (who could be inconsistent and uncontrolled) might not pose a huge threat, and that there was a danger that the group might get into competition against the threat rather than unite to think and plan how best to relate to the outside world.

These comments initially provoked — probably for the first time — quite open hostility to me and to my style, which was variously described as confronting and patronizing. I was accused of not taking charge, of not telling them what they could do to help themselves, and of just stirring things up and making them worse. I sat quiet at this point, feeling very "got at" and knowing that if I did open my mouth it would be to defend myself, which felt inappropriate. Finally, someone said she was surprised at how angry people were feeling when these issues had never been openly discussed before. She commented on how competitive the children could be and how the group was feeling in competition with parents when surely they all needed to be working together. This comment effectively dissipated the anger, and they turned to thinking about ways in which they could have regular and constructive, organized dialogues with parents rather than ad hoc intrusion. The meeting ended by someone observing, interestingly, that the way I was perceived in the school was as an "honorary Jew".

In this group meeting, the themes of inside and outside were the primary focus. Outsiders were a potential threat to be "neutralized", either by being dismissed, or by being assimilated so that any difference was denied. Uncomfortable though it was, I had to maintain a sense of my difference from both the group and from their description of management. It was very tempting to join with some of their criticisms, and almost irresistible to enjoy their "acceptance" of me as one of them. I remember it as being perhaps the most difficult moment to stay in role and maintain distance.

The session seemed to be pivotal in the life of the group. Issues of threat from the outside (which were very concretely expressed by the wall), and the need to deny difference inside in order to survive, were developed thereafter. The group began to see that many of the physical structures and procedures in the school (e.g. changing year heads and form tutors annually; discouraging mixed-age-group recreational activities whilst separating the equivalent age classes across the building; making many staff meetings voluntary but then not taking or circulating minutes) produced fragmented groups bound together by a particular shared identity (e.g. teaching subject). These shared identities were quite explicit and exclusive and seemed to serve the function of holding small groups together against external threats (be they from children, parents, colleagues, senior management, or governors). Outsiders were treated with caution (even if they were from within the institution) as they threatened to bring chaos and disintegration. None of the organization structures in the school was flexible enough to face the need of individuals and small groups for security whilst developing integrative links and some sense of collective cohesion.

EVALUATION

Evaluation of this group is difficult as it appeared to raise more questions and highlight more difficulties than it presented solutions. Although on the one hand using an "internal consultant" made the setting up of the group easy, on the other hand it made addressing some of the themes around difference (and competition) both difficult and painful. In many ways the group experienced a different type of management and authority from me, which served only to highlight their perceptions of the inadequacy of management within the school. Although I hope much of the anxiety and hostility this generated was kept within the bounds of the group, there was inevitably some envy and suspicion from other staff, and not all the group's hard-won ideas were well received. In particular this was made difficult by the headteacher, who, whilst ostensibly grateful to me, was nevertheless threatened by the way in which the group took on a thinking role within the school and by which I think he felt both challenged as well as supported. One positive outcome for me was his subsequent request for regular meetings with me to think about the school — originally focused on my role, but rapidly broadened to thinking about his own.

No structural changes resulted from this intervention; the school remained hierarchical and male-dominated. Within the membership of the group, however, there was a more permeable and fluid feel to their relations, which crossed managerial boundaries; a culture was established in which mutual support in problem solving became the norm. Although difficult to establish conclusively, I felt that this group *did* effectively model a greater tolerance of relative strengths and weaknesses for the staff as a whole.

CONCLUSIONS

The issue around my role as an "internal consultant" was critical for this group in this school. The reasons for any institution choosing an internal rather than an external consultant were invested with a religious and cultural significance as well as an institutional one in this case. Some of the general reasons might be as follows:

1. It may feel safer to keep "secrets" or difficulties within the institution.

2. It seems likely that the prospect of change is always tinged with ambivalence, for there is somewhere the hope that an internal consultant will be caught up in the belief system of the institution and that the status quo will be maintained.

3. Being "internal" *does* make challenge more difficult, as roles and relationships outside the consultation have to continue.

4. It is very difficult for any consultant to remain detached and objective during the work, but the pressures to become "assimilated" into the institution or group are particularly great on the internal consultant. The wish to be seen as the same can be perceived as a defence against a fear of disintegration and loss of identity if *differences* are openly acknowledged.

Not all the issues and concerns around my internal status were negatively charged. I felt that by trying to manage my dual role, I was given an opportunity to model different approaches and experiences involved in the various roles I had within the institution.

Having a consultant who was different but inside did mean that negative feelings and attitudes could be expressed *within* the group and that group members could survive the experience. Hopefully this led to a diminishing tendency to project negative feelings onto individuals and groups outside.

Most directly, the expansion of my role beyond individual casework was subsequently of benefit both to me and, I hope, to the school. Although impossible to measure, it was my impression that, when dealing with subsequent referrals, in fewer instances was I asked to provide solutions. It felt as if participating staff were generally less inclined to abdicate responsibility to an outside "expert" and were more inclined to think for themselves. It was as if the group had "taken in" an experience of being reflective and were then able to be "internal consultants" to themselves.

For the nine members of this group, I had little doubt that they acquired a greater sense of competence through both the learning and the support that the consultation provided. In this school, *difference* was experienced primarily negatively and was imbued with religious and cultural significance. Following the group, I felt that the participants positively valued differences between themselves and with me; thus they could acknowledge different approaches, skills, and experiences instead of feeling competitive and threatened.

Eventually, too, using feedback from the group as a vehicle, my relationship with the headteacher was considerably altered. Although the two deputies became less competitive and more supportive of each other, their relationship with the headteacher continued to be problematic. He had more difficulty in managing them by playing them off against each other, but I felt that the school benefitted as a whole from their changed relationships. Within the wider staff group, reactions were more difficult to gauge, but subsequent verbal reports led me to believe that the "work group" were more challenging in staff meetings, particularly over issues where "externals" were being blamed. Thus some other staff felt quite resentful of the group and were angry with me as a consequence. Others, however, welcomed the challenge and reported that the school seemed to be "waking up". In the longer term it felt to me as if staff were more able to support each other in the face of difficulties with children, and therefore demands on my time became more manageable.

Despite the dangers of working with only part of an institution, I feel that this group were able to take up change not only for themselves but also on behalf of the school. It was only through constant attention in the sessions to the potential divisiveness within the institution that this was made possible.

Of enormous importance to me in running this group was the regular opportunity I had to consult with a colleague. I was lucky enough to be able to discuss the content of the group sessions, the feelings they engendered in me, and my hypotheses about the impact they were making on the wider school system (gleaned from my work in the school in my other role). It felt particularly important to meet regularly as I was working alone and had no other opportunity to share my understanding as the group *developed*. Without such support I feel that I would have found it almost impossible to resist the group pressures, and my efforts to remain "outside", but understanding, would have been seriously impaired.

CHAPTER TWELVE

Old chestnuts roasted in systemic consultancy with teachers

Kirsten Blow
Chartered Psychologist and Co-Director,
Oxford Family Institute.

[This powerful case study demonstrates not only the application of a systemic framework, but also the explicit use of skills and techniques associated with this approach, such as hypothesizing, circular questioning, and reflective discussion. Negotiation of the role of researcher allowed Kirsten Blow to create an observing system in which consultant, teachers, and pupils in two schools were able to explore their understanding of teaching and learning in a new way. It shows how all concerned became curious about what had been highly redundant patterns of relationships and led to significant changes at all levels of the system in both schools concerned, not least in the reading performance of the pupils. An impressive piece of work. — Eds.]

SCOUTING

The idea for this work emerged from an interaction between the ideas that spring from the theoretical model on which Milan systemic practice is based and the challenges offered by my work as an educational psychologist.

Like many another educational psychologist, I have experienced being snared in having to choose my client as being either the pupil or the school system: on the one hand, understanding learning chiefly from the point of view of the quality of the learner and therefore getting too focused on educational diagnosis; or, on the other hand, viewing learning predominantly from a teaching point of view and therefore getting lost in a search for the correct way of teaching.

The systemic approach offered me a new way of thinking about this dilemma and a new way of exploring it. I saw a way forward that would allow me to focus on the developing pattern between teacher expectation and pupil performance, between the teacher's belief about the pupil as a learner and the pupil's response to this.

My new role as "researcher" liberated me to include myself in the system and to explore how my professional relationship had contributed to the formulation and definition of the very school systems I was attempting to help change. The consultancy thus offered me an opportunity to reflect on my own practice.

ENTRY

Two headteachers in my area were interested in using my ideas at a staff level. In one, a new headteacher was challenged by the old staff's unwillingness to implement his ideas, and, in the other, an established headteacher saw himself as having lost his chance of ever implementing his ideas and vision for his school. Both head-teachers had been involved in family/school interviews with me and had been excited by the way difficult issues could be addressed without alienating parents. They were also interested to hear about the ideas I was developing as a trainee on the Tavistock Clinic's Milan Systemic Course in Family Therapy.

CONTRACTING

A meeting was arranged with both headteachers in which I discussed my proposals. I was keen to structure the consultancy in such a way that the theoretical model was used by me not only when thinking about the problem posed by the pupils' failure to learn or when trying to understand the pupils' predicament, but also for the "research" methodology.

My proposal was as follows:

- I would construct a learning questionnaire for pupils. The questions should be designed in such a way that they invited pupils to reflect on their learning experience.

- This questionnaire would be used to interview a group of six pupils.

- The pupils would come from the lower junior classes and be chosen on the basis of their reading scores, as assessed by the Special Educational Needs advisory teachers. The pupils with the lowest scores would be selected. (The rationale for this selection came from the finding from the Bennett report that pupils who had failed to be confident readers by the age of 9 years had a very poor educational prognosis.)

- These interviews were to be videotaped.

- The videotaped interviews with the pupils were to form the basis of six sessions with the pupils' teachers and the advisory teachers; this group was referred to as the professional group.

- These sessions were to be audiotaped.

- The project should be approved by the LEA and funded by

making time available for the teachers and for me, as well as for outside supervision for me.

- Parents of the pupils involved should be informed of the pupil-interviews and invited to make comments.

The project was then discussed with the advisory teachers and with the school staff by the headteacher and me. Agreement was reached to go ahead.

DATA GATHERING

My supervisor and I met to evaluate the learning questionnaire. A series of twenty-four questions was designed. The questions invited the pupils to think about their own experience at school, what they believed their teachers thought about them, how they believed their parents viewed their successes and failures, and how they explained that some children learned faster than others. The questions ranged in nature; for example:

"If someone who was just about to start school asked you what it was about, what would you say?"

"If you made up your mind to be a good reader, who would notice it first? Last? Who would be most surprised/least surprised?"

"Who in the class would be most upset if you chose to become a good reader?"

The Special Educational Needs teacher selected the pupils after an assessment of all the pupils in the relevant age bracket, and I then carried out the interviews with the pupils.

DIAGNOSIS

We agreed that for the purpose of the meetings with school staff it was important for me to develop a whole-school hypothesis about the learning and teaching philosophy of the school. This hypothesis would inform the questions I asked in my consultancy with the teachers.

The consultancy was originally arranged as a way of exploring how systemic ideas and methodology could be used in the educational world. I particularly wanted to see if I could conduct a conversation with educators that avoided the more traditional linear explanations for failing to learn in school which often lead to someone being blamed — either the teacher/educational system or the pupil/family system. I was looking for a way forward that would facilitate a reorganized experience from which the teachers could have access to experiencing and understanding the meaning of being embedded in an ongoing feedback system. I hoped to be, at one and the same time, free to change the rules of the relationship, which would give me an opening to establish the extent to which the conversations I had had so far with the staff had maintained the idea of someone having to be blamed.

In one of the schools there was a very powerful belief in the force of parental deprivation which made it difficult for the staff to look for other explanations, or to explore how such a powerful belief influenced them as educators. I, on the other hand, had the belief that I must make the teachers see that the best (only) way to help these pupils was to focus on teaching so as to protect the pupils from yet another deprivation. I did not question whether the kind of change I was after should have been addressed at a social/political level rather than in the context of the pupil/teacher relationship. What constrained me from widening the conversation was my fear that, if I did this, it would play into the teachers' wish to look at parental deprivation, which, I thought, would distract them from addressing the one thing they did have control over, namely teaching. A stalemate was reached, and I lost my curiosity.

In the other school there had been an increase in demand for psychological assessments. I wondered if this was the teachers' response to their new headteacher's increased in-service programme for them. I saw that the more he did, the more the staff wanted me to look at the pupils to identify special needs. I was caught up in a dilemma: if I focused on teaching, it was as if I were agreeing with the head teacher; but if I engaged with the teachers in a conversation about neurological dysfunctioning, I would be labelling pupils, which was something that I wished to avoid.

In both schools there was then an urgency for me to place my focus for change in the educational relationships between teachers and pupils. This made it difficult for the teachers to challenge my ideas, and it also made it difficult for me to reflect on how the force of my beliefs shaped their conversations.

It was the strength of these redundant patterns that enabled the supervisor to understand that, as long as the conversation remained in the domain of explanations, I would be doing more of the same. To achieve a different view of the teaching/learning/consultation process, I had to abandon the domain of explanations in order to think about the process in the domain of aesthetics (Mendez et al., 1988).

The supervisor and I had the idea that by making the teachers observers to my conversations with the pupils (in which the pupils' own learning experiences and belief systems were explored), both the teachers and I could become interested in and curious about the relationship between what the children thought the teachers thought about them as learners, and how the teachers taught. We were less clear about how this process would inform me about my conversation with the teachers.

PLANNING

I made it explicit to the teachers before I met with them that these meetings were as much for my benefit as for theirs — perhaps more so, as I had for some time been preoccupied with understanding how pupils develop ideas about themselves as learners, and about how these ideas then affected future learning and teaching.

This input changed the usual pattern between the school staff and myself. Up to this point, consultancy had run along the lines of the teachers having the problems and I the answers, or at least suggested solutions to the problem of pupils' under-achievement. Although we had a mutual respect for each other, these previous interactions had never been very successful. I had the experience that the only solution acceptable to the staff was to change the plight of the families or provide extra resources or recommend transfer to other schools. The staff, on the other hand, experienced these sessions as a criticism of their teaching. This left everyone feeling disempowered and resigned to the status quo.

On this occasion, I made it explicit that I had no ready-made solution and no hidden agenda on new teaching methods. This enabled a new relationship to develop based on the ethos of a team pursuing new insights into the learning process and being prepared to experiment for the sake of gaining new information.

I decided to use the first session with the teachers to ask them, firstly, to answer the questions as they would have when they were 9 years old, and, secondly, to think about pupils from their perspective as teachers — that is, from a professional point of view.

I also decided that, in the last session, most of the time should be used to reflect on the previous five sessions.

INTERVENTION

My videotaped conversations with the pupils provided the teachers with new information about their pupils. This information did not always favour the story the teachers had about the pupils. When this happened it offered both the teachers and me an opportunity to be curious about how the story had come about, what maintained it, and, last but not least, how this story affected the teaching/ learning relationship and how the teaching/learning relationship affected the story.

The intervention was thus: to locate the consultancy in the context of the narrative mode, where the powers of the dominant story could be suspended while exceptions to the story were being pursued. This move freed both the teachers and me to relate as co-authors (and therefore also to suspend for the time being the dominant story about our relationship). It also gave us an opportunity to talk about what happened when explanations were elevated to causes and became a reality (White, 1988).

When the teachers and I looked at the video of the pupils' conversation with me, we were, of course, not only able to hear their pupils talk about their understanding of themselves as learners, they were also able to observe me at work. This opened a space for them to question my interaction with their pupils: for example, why I asked certain questions rather than others. They also became curious about my professional beliefs and practice and made comments about how much more helpful these conversations were than my past involvement with them. It was when this happened that conversations about professional relationship became possible. This sense of being in a new, more egalitarian relationship enabled me to be less interested in making the teachers see that these children could learn much more than they believed, and it engaged us all to be interested in how patterns of interaction became self-fulfilling prophecies.

On the whole, the questions that engaged the teachers most were those that explored their relationship with their pupils. For example, the pupils' response to the questions, "If your teacher were here what do you think he/she would say you were best at? " and "How do you think teachers find out what you are best at?", gave rise to the following discussion:

> Most of the pupils in one of the schools thought that their
> teacher would say they were best at reading. It was difficult for
> them to think about how teachers found out what pupils were
> good at, but a consensus emerged that probably this came about
> when teachers went around and looked at their work, as they
> would then say, "Well done!"

An extract from the conversation the teachers had after they had seen this part of the video is presented below. To begin with, the conversation centred on one pupil who had had severe behaviour problems. Teacher A started by giving an account of how she had successfully dealt with this. She described how she challenged his behaviour by setting norms and being explicit about what was and what was not acceptable in her classroom. I linked this successful experience to decisions that his present teacher, teacher B, was now faced with over how to approach the boy's serious learning difficulty. Teacher A was very worried that if her original approach were carried over into the learning situation, then the boy might be destroyed.

> A: "It makes you wonder, but then I would not have the nerve,
>   or to me it appears the nerve, to totally destroy him."
> B: "You do not know. I am not sure. I do not think I would
>   have said this a couple of weeks ago, but the more we have
>   talked about this, this deception, about what is going on
>   between us and the children, the more I feel we are doing
>   them a disservice."

Teacher C then gave an account of how she had changed her approach to a child since our last meeting by telling the pupil that she knew that he could do better.

D: "I have suddenly begun to think that we spend so much time, and I have always thought we were right, in doing this, in building these children's confidence. We feel we must give these children a better self-image by praising them, and then suddenly they have all got this lovely self-image and nothing is happening. They are not working. I am beginning to think that this kind of self-image is not everything."

B: "This is fascinating. We have never been discussing this before."

Everyone agreed; "wonderful", they all echoed.

The conversation continued to come back to how to give pupils feedback on their performance. The preferred solution was to praise, as anything else was seen as destroying this kind of pupil. Observing on the video how much awareness the pupils had about this process helped the teachers to question this.

B: "The problem is, we do not encourage competition. It is not done for children to compete against each other. Against oneself, yes, but how do you encourage this in a young child?"

D: "In the old-fashioned days you had a list. If you were bottom of the list you were in a pretty poor state. If you were top, then the child could sit back and enjoy it. We do not have a list like that so a child cannot read it."

B: "But they are not aware of that, as we discovered with Gill last year. We asked her how good she was, and she said she was very good at reading. We said, "What makes you think that?" And she said, "Well, I am top of the list". But in fact it was an inverted list; my children went to the bottom as they improved."

A: "So do mine."

B: "Yes, so I have changed my list around. Because she saw her name up there at the top that meant top for her in the class."

Me: "So, perhaps what we are talking about is: how do we know how pupils understand our feedback about learning?"

C: "I do not know if we need to ignore competition for children to cope?"

A: "No, there is an awful lot of this."

B: "But we are not concerned about those, are we? They are not the children we worry over and spend time over."

C: "But you know sometimes I wonder whether Gill gets reinforced at home. It's so complacent. She may say, "Let me go on to things where I have to compete, I like my ice-skating where I get badges". Well, it is interesting. When she is put in a competitive situation she is striving all the time and, since, her reading has gathered momentum. This really surprises me, considering she was a child who, when she came to me, could read only three or four words. This is the fourth term I have had her in my class."

D;   "The fourth term?"

C: "Now she has a reading ability, well I think it is coming on, probably near to her age because, yes, suddenly it began to click and now she is becoming a bit more competitive since she has become aware, and it is interesting, she does not say these things, but she is in the classroom being aware perhaps of the pecking order of whether you hear people read when I do reading pairs or whether you are one of the ones who are *heard* reading."

The teachers' belief that they could prevent the pupils from evaluating themselves and making their own sense out of their learning experiences was gradually unpicked. This led to their deciding to make small changes in their expectations of the children. It also made them much more curious about the children, and they brought many anecdotes to the sessions of conversations they had with their pupils about how they understood school and learning.

It was as if the teachers had an experience of the meaning and implications of being part of an ongoing feedback system.

EVALUATION

When tapping multiple views, it is possible to enrich and expand the picture of how complex systems function. The richness that emerges is sometimes overwhelming and can be particularly daunting when one reflects on the connections between changes in the different parts of the system, which is potentially infinite. I have chosen to evaluate the consultancy by looking:

1. At the kind of conversations that emerged between the teachers and me.

2. At a change in the relationship between the teachers and me. If the conversations had made a difference, would it not also change our expectations of each other?

3. At learning output. If the consultancy had an effect on the teachers, how would this inform the teaching/learning relationship? If, as I hoped, the teachers would begin to expect more of their pupils, would they also learn more? Seen from a different angle, if I began to feel less passionate that it was up to the teachers to rescue these children from educational failure, how would this affect learning output?

4. At my ideas about my work.

1.   The extract from the audio material is an example of a change in attitude among the teachers that took place during our conversations. There were other examples, too, where teachers suddenly saw the fit between their actions and their pupils' responses. When this happened, the teachers became engaged in finding new solutions, and there was a reported increase in learning output. This was confirmed by the teachers when they met with me three months after the last session.

There was also a difference in the kind of conversation I had with the teachers in my last sessions with them. In these sessions the use of feedback was being aired. This happened first when the teachers commented on how constrained they felt about talking to the teachers in the infant department about the pupils who had moved into the junior department. They sensed that such a conversation would be seen as criticism. It happened again when one of the teachers linked this to an experience she had when she overheard comments in the staff room about pupils she had previously taught. When this happened, she felt that such casual remarks made it difficult for them to have professional conversations about pupils' educational history, as they believed that such conversations would lead to their being judged wanting. It happened last when the teachers began to be more questioning of my conversation with the children.

They became interested in what I would have learned if I had seen the pupils individually rather than in a group, and they gave me information about the children that had not been picked up in my conversation with them. They also questioned the questions, in terms of the information they gave them as teachers. At the end of the session, the conversation focused on a different kind of consultancy in which the teachers and I would work as a team from the start.

The format of the consultancy offered a space for reflection, and, as this was not a problem-solving exercise, the rules of the relationship changed. It became possible to explore how the belief in the need for someone to be blamed had affected not only my professional relationship with the school, but also the professional relationship between the teachers, and between the teachers and the pupils. The intervention, with its focus on giving the teachers feedback about their pupils' own ideas about themselves as learners, made feedback the highest context marker. This move enabled us to explore what happens when relationships develop in such a way that no new information can be made available.

2.   In both schools the teachers wanted me to use these ideas at a whole-school level.

In one school I was invited back to run an in-service day aimed at facilitating the whole staff in planning in-service training for the following year. I understood this to be a creative move, which they hoped would address the relationship between the headteacher's view of their competence and their view of the pupils' competence. In the other school, there was a suggestion that the technique itself could be used to facilitate the interaction between teachers in the infant and junior departments of the school.

3.   The Special Educational Needs teachers reported that there had been a significant increase in most of the pupils' reading scores, encouraging us to think that enough new information was made available during the consultancy for change to take place.

4.   The experience that I gained from this project enabled me to be more confident in my interactions with teachers. I gained a greater understanding of the dilemmas that teachers face daily and yet felt at ease with myself for not having ready-made answers to them. This helped to minimize blaming relationships or relationships based on professional stereotypes.

Because of the excitement the project generated in a wider context, it also gave me more confidence in making public use of systemic ideas and methodology in the world of education.

* * *

Reflecting on the consultancy, I think that if I had worked with a team, more creative use could have been made of the richness of information gained by engaging at so many different levels. In my conversations with the teachers this would have offered a new perspective on our relationship and perhaps empowered the teachers to be more challenging of me.

It would also have given me greater confidence in myself; I was often left wondering whether I was missing opportunities or making mistakes.

CONCLUSION

The way in which children's attitudes affect the teaching they receive is an issue largely ignored in the educational debate. This consultancy offered an opportunity to explore the recursive pattern in the interaction between pupils and teachers and how a change at one level might affect learning output.

The question that remains for me and my supervisor is how to create an environment in which such a change can be maintained and developed.

Author's Note: The ideas discussed in this chapter arose out of the inspiring supervision offered by Dr. Caroline Lindsey.

Lessons learned

T hree parts of the public sector; many contexts; nine different
stories — what do they have in common, and what have we
learned from them?

The emphasis on management, personal responsibility, the
purchaser/provider split, and the need to increase organizational
effectiveness within cost limits were apparent in the case studies
from all parts of the public sector. The theme of competition between parts of the public sector was not so apparent, but perhaps it
was "bubbling underneath". It seems to us that any case study
describing internal consultancy is like a piece of broken mirror,
which will inevitably contain and therefore reflect the context. Indeed, if a work appears not to be reflecting current organizational
pressures within the public sector, one would want to ask "Why
not?" and become very curious about how this organization had
somehow become cut off from the wider picture.

Despite pressures on time and more constrained roles within
the purchaser/provider culture, our authors show that it has been
possible to engage in consultancy within their own organizations.
Not only has it been possible, but it has also been beneficial in

many ways, as they clearly show in the evaluation of their work. It is refreshing to find that this is the case despite concern that consultancy is the kind of work that might get squeezed out of professional roles.

As to differences between the case studies, some represent formal, contracted pieces of work (e.g. Emilia Dowling, Liz Kennedy, and Martin Wrench), whereas others are more informal (e.g. Robin Burgess). For some internal consultants, the request for help came to them clearly within the framework of another role in the organization, and it may not ever have been framed as consultancy, although approached in a consultative style. For others, there was no explicit request but a wish on the part of the consultant to reframe a part of their work in this way.

Some consultants were working with individuals, others worked with groups, and some were able to work with larger organizational units or the whole organization.

Many of our case studies showed the importance of being able to negotiate consultancy as a different, extra role in the organization — to avoid being seen as just an "extra pair of hands" and to feel that the work is legitimized within the organization.

It seems important to be able to create a space to explore expectations of the work requested — and that missing out this stage can lead to difficulties later on. As we have seen, the sorts of issues that might need to be clarified are:

1. The difference it makes to be internal as opposed to external to the organization; the expected losses and gains.
2. The relationship with other roles in the organization: where these can be complementary and where conflicting.
3. The responsibility and involvement of one's own line management, as well as the responsibility and involvement of the line management of all those involved in the consultancy.

We have already discussed the difficulties of creating the kind of stance needed by the internal consultant to bring about change and also possible evidence of "slippage" from this position.

It may be that the crucial factor in positioning oneself as a consultant within the organization is not so much that *we* can continue to feel curious, but that we can create a context in which our *clients* can feel curious enough to work with us.

We expected that the internal consultants in the case studies might have difficulties in negotiating "withdrawal" from the consultancy process. We thought that the consultants might feel a pull to continue the process beyond the agreed contract; that de-roling might actually have the effect of throwing others back into role again, in a kind of never-ending process (Huffington & Fisher, 1991). However, what we discovered is that most of our authors did not describe any particular problems with re-entry, in contrast to the sometimes huge struggles around entry. Many authors reported that the consultancy work had a facilitating effect on their roles in the organization.

It seems that, for our authors, opening the consultancy brief appeared to mean that it remained open as an option for future work and that the performance of other roles in the organization were enriched as a result.

It is pleasing to note that all case studies report at least some positive changes at individual, group, or whole organization level and sometimes at all three levels. A wide variety of approaches and methods were used by the authors within the context of consultancy, from informal discussion, teaching events, and group work to more formal systemic interviewing techniques. The case studies demonstrate the wide variety of approaches that can be used within a systemic framework, explicit or otherwise.

We asked all our authors to consider evaluation and outcome and, as we have seen, all of them report some positive change. However, despite the audit culture in the public sector, few of them reported that they had discussed evaluation at the planning stage and few used formal audit or outcome measures. We would like to suggest that this is the next area of development for internal consultants. This is essential in order that their services can be seen as integral to the work of the organization rather than the invisible part of the iceberg, and also that the work of internal consultants continues to be legitimized.

One of the most interesting aspects of our work as editors has been the process of facilitating, through this book, the transition to the outside world of what was internal to an organization. Confidentiality is a very important issue, and all our authors have needed to go through sometimes complex processes of negotiation to obtain legitimacy for going public with their work. In this sense, they have often found themselves revisiting the struggles around negotiating the original piece of work — that is, creating a new context for the consultancy.

One further point to reiterate is the need for the internal consultant to find support by obtaining "consultancy to the consultant". This can be achieved through informal links within and outside the organization: setting up support groups, joining professional organizations (e.g. CPOC[1]), or participating in training courses. It is important that the benefits to organizations from internal consultants are maximized by giving this role adequate recognition and support.

Our parting message is our shared belief in internal consultancy as the way forward for many organizational problems facing public sector agencies.

The elegant and appropriate use of internal consultancy can lead to creative and relevant solutions being found by those who are most affected when things go wrong — and therefore are likely to benefit most when things go well.

NOTE

1. Clinical Psychology and Organizational Consultancy Group (CPOC). National interest group of clinical, educational, and occupational psychologists. Contact address: Anthea Keller, Department of Clinical Psychology, 43 Kings Close, Watford, WD1 8UB. Telephone: 0923 680731.

REFERENCES

Andersen, T. (1984). Consultation: would you like co-evolution instead of referral? *Family Systems Medicine, 2* (4): 370–379.

Anderson, H., & Goolishian, H. (1986). Systems with agencies dealing with domestic violence. In L. C. Wynne, S. H. McDaniel, & T. T. Weber (Eds.), *Systems Consultation: A New Perspective for Family Therapy*. New York: Guildford.

Anderson H., & Goolishian, H. (1988). Human systems as linguistic systems: preliminary and evolving ideas about the implications for clinical theory. *Family Process, 27* (4): 371–393.

Argyris, C. (1973). *Intervention Theory and Method: A Behavioural Science View*. Reading, MA: Addison Wesley.

Bachrach, L. L. (1978). A conceptual approach to de-institutionalisation. *Hospital and Community Psychiatry, 29*: 573–578.

Bateson, G. (1973). *Steps to an Ecology of Mind*. St. Albans: Paladin.

Bennun, I. (1986). Evaluating family therapy: a comparison of the Milan and problem-solving approaches *Journal of Family Therapy, 8* (3): 235–242.

Bianco, V. E. (1985). The internal consultant and the eternal struggle. *Training & Development Journal, 39* (7) (July): 51–53

Bor, R., & Miller, R. (1991). *Internal Consultation in Health Care Settings*. London: Karnac Books.

163

Brunning, H., Cole, C., & Huffington, C. (1990). *The Change Directory: Key Issues in Organizational Development and the Management of Change*. Leicester: The BPS (DCP).

Brunning, H., & Huffington, C. (1990). Jumping off the fence: developing the consultancy model. *Clinical Psychology Forum, 29*: 31–33.

Brunning, H., & Huffington, C. (1991). After the jump—what next? The thrills and spills of internal consultancy. *Clinical Psychology Forum, 35*: 33–35.

Campbell, D., Draper, R., & Huffington, C. (1991a). *Second Thoughts on the Theory and Practice of the Milan Approach to Family Therapy*. London: Karnac Books.

Campbell, D., Draper, R., & Huffington, C. (1991). *A Systemic Approach to Consultation*. London: Karnac Books.

Carr, A. (1991). Milan systemic family therapy: a review of ten empirical investigations. *Journal of Family Therapy, 13* (3): 237–266.

Cecchin, G. (1987). Hypothesizing, circularity and neutrality revisited: an invitation to curiosity. *Family Process, 26*: 405–413.

Covin, T. J., & Kilmann, R. H. (1990a). Implementation of large scale planned change: some areas of agreement and disagreement. *Psychological Reports, 66* (3, Part 2) (June): 1235–1241.

Covin, T. J., & Kilmann, R. H. (1990b). Participant perceptions of positive and negative influences on large scale change. *Group and Organization Studies, 15* (2): 233–248.

Department of Health (1990). *The National Health Service and Community Care Act*. London: HMSO.

Deys, C., Dowling, E., & Golding, V. (1989). Clinical psychology: a consultative approach in general practice. *Journal of the Royal College of General Practitioners, 39*: 342–344.

Fruggeri, L., Dotti, D., Ferrari, R., & Matteini, M. (1985). The systemic approach in a mental health service In D. Campbell & R. Draper (Eds), *Applications of Systemic Family Therapy: The Milan Approach*. London: Grune & Stratton.

Goldner, V. (1988). Generation and gender: normative and covert hierarchies. *Family Process, 27*: 17–31.

Green, R. J., & Herget, M. (1989a). Outcomes of systemic/strategic team consultation. I: Overview and one month's results. *Family Process, 28*: 37–58.

Green, R. J., & Herget, M. (1989b). Outcomes of systemic/strategic team consultation. II: Three year follow-up and a theory of "emergent design". *Family Process, 28*: 417–437.

Handy, C. (1981). *Understanding Organizations*. London: Penguin.

Harrison, E. G., & Robertson, M. J. (1985). O.D.: an alternative strategy for organizational renewal in the N.H.S.? *Hospital and Health Services Review*: 125–129.

Hoffman, L. (1985). Beyond power and control: toward a "second order" family systems therapy. *Family Systems Medicine, 3* (4): 381–396. [Also in *Exchanging Voices*. London: Karnac Books, 1993.]

Hoffman, L. (1988). A constructivist position for family therapy. *Irish Journal of Psychology, 9* (1): 110–129. [Also in *Exchanging Voices*. London: Karnac Books, 1993.]

Huffington, C., & Fisher, J. (1991). The "bringing forth" of learning. *Context* (7) (Winter 1990–1991): 22–27

Lippitt, G., & Lippitt, K. (1978). *The Consulting Process in Action*. La Jolla, CA: University Associates.

Mashal, M., Feldman, R. N., & Sigal, J. J. (1989). The unravelling of a treatment paradigm: a follow-up study of the Milan approach to family therapy. *Family Process, 28*: 457–470.

Mendez, C. L., Coddou, F., & Maturana, H. (1988). The bringing forth of pathology. *Irish Journal of Psychology* (Special Issue: Constructivism).

Menzies-Lyth, I. (1959). The functioning of social systems as a defence against anxiety. Reprinted in I. Menzies-Lyth, *Containing Anxiety in Institutions*. London: Free Association, 1988.

Nufrio, P. M. (1983). Diary of a mad internal consultant. *Group and Organization Studies, 8* (1) (March): 7–18

Ovretveit, J. (1992). *Health Service Quality: An Introduction to Quality Measurement for Health Services*. Oxford: Blackwell Special Projects.

Ovretveit, J., Brunning, H., & Huffington, C. (1992). Adapt or decay: why clinical psychologists must develop the consulting role. *Clinical Psychology Forum, 46*: 27–29.

Pace, L. A., & Argona, D. R. (1989). Participatory action research: a view from Xerox. *American Behavioural Scientist, 32* (5) (May-June): 552–565.

Penn, P., & Scheinberg, M. (1986). Is there therapy after consultation? In L. C. Wynne, S. H. McDaniel, & T.T. Weber, *Systems Consultation: A New Perspective for Family Therapy*. New York: Guilford Press.

Roberts, M., Caesar, L., Perryclear, B., & Phillips, D. (1989). Reflecting team consultations. *Journal of Strategic and Systemic Therapies, 8*: 38–46.

Selvini-Palazzoli, M. (1980). The problem of the referring person. *Journal of Marital and Family Therapy, 6* (1): 3–9.

Von Foerster, H. (1979). Cybernetics of cybernetics. In K. Krippendorff, (Ed.), *Communication and Control*. New York: Gordon & Beach.

White, M. (1988). The externalising of the problem and the reauthoring of lives and relationships. *Dulwich Centre Newsletter*: 8–14.

Williams, A. (1989). The problem of the referring person in consultancy. *Journal of Strategic and Systemic Therapies, 8* (2 & 3): 16–21.

Winn, A. (1973). Change agents, scapegoats, power and love. *Group Process, 5* (2): 153–160.

INDEX